The Wild Turkey and Its Hunting

Edward A. McIlhenny

INTRODUCTION

Although many eminent naturalists and observers have written of the turkey from the date of its introduction to European civilization to the present time, there has been no very satisfactory history of the intimate life of this bird, nor has there been a satisfactory analysis of either the material from which our fossil turkeys are known, or the many writings concerning the early history of the bird and its introduction to civilization. I have attempted in this work to cover the entire history of this very interesting and vanishing game bird, and believe it will fill a long-felt want of hunters and naturalists for a more detailed description of its life history.

This work was begun by Chas. L. Jordan and would have been completed by him, except for his untimely death in 1909.

Mr. Jordan for more than sixty years was a careful observer and lover of the wild turkey, and for many years the study of this bird occupied almost his entire time. I feel safe in saying that Mr. Jordan knew more of the ways of the wild turkey in the wilds than any man who ever lived. No more convincing example of his patience and perseverance in his study of the bird can be given than the accompanying photographs, all of which were taken of the wild birds in the big outdoors by Mr. Jordan.

At the time of Mr. Jordan's death he was in his sixty-seventh year and was manager of the Morris game preserve of over 10,000 acres, near Hammond, La. He had been most successful in attracting to this preserve a great abundance of game, and was very active in suppressing poaching and illegal hunting. His activity in this cause brought about his death, as he was shot in the back by a poacher during the afternoon of February 24, 1909, for which Allen Lagrue, his murderer, is now serving a life sentence in the penitentiary.

I had known Mr. Jordan for a number of years before his death and was much interested in his work with the turkey, as I, for years, had been carrying on similar studies. After Mr. Jordan's death, through the kindness of Mr. John K. Renaud, I secured his notes, manuscript, and photographic plates of the wild turkey, and with these, and my knowledge of the bird, I have attempted to compile a work I think he would have approved.

Mr. Jordan from time to time wrote articles on the wild turkey for sporting magazines, among them *Shooting and Fishing*, and parts of his articles are brought into the present publication. I have carried out the story of the wild turkey as if told by Mr. Jordan, as his full notes on the bird enable me to do this.

I am indebted to Dr. R. W. Shufeldt for his chapter on the fossil turkey, the introduction of the turkey to civilization, and photographs accompanying his two chapters, written at my request especially for this work.

E. A. M.

THE WILD TURKEY AND ITS HUNTING

CHAPTER I
MY EARLY TRAINING WITH THE TURKEYS

My father was a great all-round hunter and pioneer in the state of Alabama, once the paradise of hunters. He was particularly devoted to deer hunting and fox hunting, owning many hounds and horses. He knew the ways and haunts of the forest people and from him my brothers and I got our early training in woodcraft. I was the youngest of three sons, all of whom were sportsmen to the manner born. My brothers and myself were particularly fond of hunting the wild turkey, and were raised and schooled in intimate association with this noble bird; the fondness for this sport has remained with me through life. I therefore may be pardoned when I say that I possess a fair knowledge of their language, their habits, their likes and dislikes.

In the great woods surrounding our home there were numbers of wild turkeys, and I can well remember my brother Frank's skill in calling them. Every spring as the gobbling season approached my brothers and myself would construct various turkey calls and lose no opportunity for practising calling the birds. I can recall, too, when but a mere lad, coming down from my room in the early morning to the open porch, and finding assembled the family and servants, including the little darkies and the dogs, all in a state of great excitement. I hastened to learn the cause of this and was shown with admiration a big gobbler, and as I looked at the noble bird, with its long beard and glossy plumage, lying on the porch, I felt it was a beautiful trophy of the chase.

"Who killed it?" I asked. "Old Massa, he kill 'im," came from the mouths of half a dozen excited little darkies. A few days later my brothers brought in other turkeys. This made me long for the time when I would be old enough to hunt this bird, and these happy incidents inspired me with ambition to acquire proficiency in turkey hunting, and to learn every method so that I might excel in that sport.

As I grew older, but while still a mere lad, I would often steal to the woods in early morning on my way to school, and, hiding myself in some thick bush, sitting with my book in my lap and a rude cane joint or bone of a turkey's wing for a call in my hand, I would watch for the turkeys. When they appeared I would study every movement of the birds, note their call, yelp, cluck, or gobble, and I gradually learned each sound they made had its meaning. I would study closely the ways of the hens and their conduct toward the young and growing broods; I would also note their attention to the old or young gobblers, and the mannerisms of the male birds toward the females. All this time I would be using my call, attempting to imitate every note that the turkeys made, and watching the effect. These were my rudimentary and earliest lessons in turkey lore and lingo, and what I have often called my schooling with the turkeys.

At this age I had not begun the use of a rifle or shotgun on turkeys, although I had killed smaller game, such as squirrels, rabbits, ducks, and quail. I was sixteen years of age when I began to hunt the wild turkeys. I discovered then that although I was able to do good calling I had much more to learn to cope successfully with the wily ways of this bird. It took years of the closest observation and study to acquire the knowledge which later made me a successful turkey hunter, and I have gained this knowledge only after tramping over thousands of miles of wild territory, through swamps and hummocks, over hills and rugged mountain sides, through deep gulches, quagmires, and cane brakes, and spending many hours in fallen treetops, behind logs or other natural cover, not to be observed, but to observe, by day and by night, in rain, wind, and storm. I have hunted the wild turkeys on the great prairies and thickets of Texas, along the open river bottoms of the Brazos, Colorado, Trinity, San Jacinto, Bernardo, as well as the rivers, creeks, hills, and valleys of Alabama, Florida, Mississippi, and Louisiana. With all modesty, I believe I have killed as many old gobblers with patriarchal beards as any man in the world. I do not wish to say this boastfully, but present it as illustrative of the experience I have had with these birds, and particularly with old gobblers, for I have always found a special delight in outwitting the wary old birds.

I doubt not many veteran turkey hunters have in mind some old gobbler who seemed invincible; some bird that had puzzled them for three or four years without their learning the tricks of the cunning fellow. Perhaps in these pages there may be found some information which will enable even the old hunter to better circumvent the bird. I am aware that there are times when the keenest sportsmen will be outwitted, often when success seems assured.

How well I know this. Many times I have called turkeys to within a few feet of me; so near that I have heard their "put-put." And they would walk away without my getting a shot. Often does this occur to the best turkey hunter, on account of the game approaching from the rear, or other unexpected point, and suddenly without warning fly or run away. No one can avoid this, but the sportsman who understands turkeys can exercise care and judgment and kill his bird, where others unacquainted with the bird fail. I believe I can take any man or boy who possesses a good eye and fair sense, and in one season make a good turkey hunter of him. I know of many nefarious tricks by which turkeys could be easily secured, but I shall not tell of any method of hunting and capturing turkeys but those I consider sportsmanlike. Although an ardent turkey hunter, I have too much respect for this glorious bird to see it killed in any but an honorable way. The turkey's fate is hard enough as it is. The work of destruction goes on from year to year, and the birds are being greatly reduced in numbers in many localities. The extinction of them in some states has already been accomplished, and in others it is only a matter of time; but there are many localities in the South and West, especially in the Gulf-bordering states, where they are still plentiful, and with any sort of protection will remain so. Some of these localities are so situated that they will for generations remain primeval forests, giving ample shelter and food to the turkey.

A novice might think it an easy matter to find turkeys after seeing their tracks along the banks of streams or roads, or in the open field, where they lingered the day before. But these birds are not likely to be in the same place the following day; they will probably be some miles away on a leafy ridge, scratching up the dry leaves and mould in quest of insects and acorns, or in some cornfield gleaning the scattered grain; or perhaps they might be lingering on the banks of some small stream in a dense swamp, gathering snails or small crustacea and water-loving insects.

To be successful in turkey hunting you must learn to rise early in the morning, ere there is a suspicion of daylight. At such a time the air is chilly, perhaps it looks like rain, and on awakening you are likely to yawn, stretch, and look at the time. Unless you possess the ardor of a sportsman it is not pleasant to rise from a comfortable bed at this hour and go forth into the chill morning air that threatens to freeze the marrow in your bones. But it is essential that you rise before light, and if you are a born turkey hunter you will soon forget the discomforts. It has been my custom, when intending to go turkey hunting, never to hesitate a moment, but, on awakening in the morning, bound out of bed at once and dress as soon as possible. It has also been my custom to calculate the distance I am to go, so as to reach the turkey range by the time or a little before day breaks. I have frequently risen at one or two o'clock in the morning and ridden twelve miles or more before daybreak for the chance to kill an old gobbler.

Early morning from the break of day until nine o'clock is the very best time during the whole day to get turkeys; but the half hour after daybreak is really worth all the rest of the day; this is the time when everything chimes with the new-born day; all life is on the move; diurnal tribes awakening from night's repose are coming into action, while nocturnal creatures are seeking their retreats. Hence at this hour there is a conglomeration of animal life and a babel of mingled sounds not heard at any other time of day. This is the time to be in the depths of the forest in quest of the wild turkey, and one should be near their roosting place if possible, quietly listening and watching every sound and motion. If in the autumn or winter you are near such a place, you are likely to hear, as day breaks, the awakening cluck at long intervals; then will follow the long, gentle, quavering call or yelp of the mother hen, arousing her sleeping brood and making known to them that the time has arrived for leaving their roosts. If in the early spring, you will listen for the salutation of the old gobbler.

CHAPTER II
RANGE, VARIATION, AND NAME

When America was discovered the wild turkey inhabited the wooded portion of the entire country, from the southern provinces of Canada and southern Maine, south to southern Mexico, and from Arizona, Kansas, and Nebraska, east to the Atlantic Ocean and the Gulf of Mexico. As the turkey is not a migratory bird in the sense that migration is usually interpreted, and while the range of the *species* is one of great extent, as might be expected, owing to the operation of the usual causes, a number of *subspecies* have resulted. At the present time, ornithologists recognize four of these as occurring within the limits of the United States, as set forth in Chapter IV beyond.

In countries thickly settled, as in the one where I now write, there is a great variety of wild turkeys scattered about in the woods of the small creeks and hills. Many hybrid wild turkeys are killed here every year. The cause of this is: every old gobbler that dares to open its mouth to gobble in the spring is within the hearing of farmers, negroes, and others, and is a marked bird. It is given no rest until it is killed; hence there are few or no wild turkeys to take care of the hens, which then visit the domestic gobbler about the farm-yards. Hence this crossing with the wild one is responsible for a great variety of plumages.

I once saw a flock of hybrids while hunting squirrels in Pelahatchie swamp, Mississippi, as I sat at the root of a tree eating lunch, about one o'clock, with gun across my lap, as I never wish to be caught out of reach of my gun. Suddenly I heard a noise in the leaves, and on looking in that direction I saw a considerable flock of turkeys coming directly toward me in a lively manner, eagerly searching for food. The moment these birds came in sight I saw they had white tips to their tails, but they had the form and action of the wild turkey, and it at once occurred to me that they were a lot of mixed breeds, half wild, half tame, with the freedom of the former. I noticed also among them one that was nearly white and one old gobbler that was a pure wild turkey; but it was too far off to shoot him. Dropping the lunch and grasping the gun was but the work of a second; then the birds came round the end of the log and began scratching under a beech tree for nuts. Seeing two gobblers put their heads together at about forty yards from me, I fired, killing both. The flock flew and ran in all directions. One hen passed within twenty paces of me and I killed it with the second barrel. A closer examination of the dead birds convinced me that there had been a cross between the wild and the tame turkeys. The skin on their necks and heads was as yellow as an orange, or more of a buckskin, buff color, while the caruncles on the neck were tinged with vermilion, giving them a most peculiar appearance; all three of those slain had this peculiar marking, and there was not a shadow of the blue or purple of the wild turkey about their heads, while all other points, save the white-tipped feathers, indicated the wild blood.

Shortly after the foregoing incident, while a party of gentlemen, including my brother, were hunting some five miles below the same creek, they flushed a flock of wild turkeys, scattering them; one of the party killed four of them that evening, two of which (hens) were full-blood wild ones. One of the remaining two, a fine gobbler, had as red a head as any tame gobbler, and the tips of the tail and rump coverts were white. The other bird (a hen) was also a half-breed. There was no buff on their heads and necks, but the purple and blue of the wild blood was apparent.

Early the next morning my brother went to the place where the turkeys were scattered the previous afternoon, and began to call. Very soon he had a reply, and three fine gobblers came running to him, when he killed two, one with each barrel; now these were full-blood wild ones.

I have noted that a number of wild turkeys in the Brazos bottoms are very different in some respects from the turkeys of the piney woods in the eastern section of that state. In Trinity County, Texas, I found the largest breed of wild turkeys I have found anywhere, but in the Brazos bottoms the gobblers which I found there in 1876, in great abundance, were of a smaller stature, but more chunky or bulky. Their gobble was hardly like that of a wild turkey, the sound resembling the gobble of a turkey under a barrel, a hoarse, guttural rumble, quite different in tone from the clear, loud, rolling gobble of

12

his cousin in the Trinity country. The gobblers of the Brazos bottoms were also distinguishable by their peculiar beards. In other varieties of turkeys three inches or less of the upper end of the beard is grayish, while those of the Brazos bottoms were more bunchy and black up to the skin of the breast. There is a variety of turkeys in the San Jacinto region, in the same state, which is quite slender, dark in color, and has a beard quite thin in brush, but long and picturesque. His gobble is shrill. This section is a low plain, generally wet in the spring, partly timbered and partly open prairie. It is a great place for the turkey.

Since the days of Audubon it has been prophesied that the wild turkey would soon become extinct. I am glad to say that the prophecies have not been realized up to the present time, even with the improved implements of destruction and great increase of hunters. There is no game that holds its own so well as the wild turkey. This is particularly true in the southern Gulf States, where are to be found heavily timbered regions, which are suited to the habits of this bird. Here shelter is afforded and an ample food supply is provided the year round. In the states of Florida, Alabama, Mississippi, North Carolina, Georgia, Louisiana, Texas, Arkansas, Missouri, and the Indian Territory the wild turkey is still to be found in reasonable abundance, and if these states will protect them by the right sort of laws, I am of the opinion that the birds will increase rapidly, despite the encroachment of civilization and the war waged upon them by sportsmen. It is not the legitimate methods of destruction that decimate the turkey ranks, as is the case with the quail and grouse, but it is the nefarious tricks the laws in many states permit, namely, trapping and baiting. The latter is by far the most destructive, and is practised by those who kill turkeys for the market, and frequently by those who want to slaughter these birds solely for count. No creature, however prolific, can stand such treatment long. The quail, though shot in great numbers by both sportsmen and market hunters, and annually destroyed legitimately by the thousands, stands it better than the wild turkey, although the latter produces and raises almost as many young at a time as the quail.

There are two reasons for this: one is, the quail are not baited and shot on the ground; the other reason is that every bobwhite in the spring can, and does, use his call, thus bringing to him a mate; but the turkey, if he dares to gobble, no matter if he is the only turkey within a radius of forty miles, has every one who hears him and can procure a gun, after him, and they pursue him relentlessly until he is killed. Among the turkeys the hens raised are greatly in excess of the gobblers. This fact seems to have been provided for by nature in making the male turkey polygamous; but as the male turkey is, during the spring, a very noisy bird, continually gobbling and strutting to attract his harem, and as he is much larger and more conspicuous than the hens, it is only natural that he is in more danger of being killed. Suppose the proportion of gobblers in the beginning of the spring is three to fifteen hens, in a certain stretch of woods. As soon as the mating season begins, these gobblers will make their whereabouts known by their noise; result—the gunners are after them at once, and the chances are ten to one they will all be killed. The hens will then have no mate and no young will be produced; whereas, if but one gobbler were left, each of our supposed fifteen hens would raise an average of ten young each, and we would also have 150 new turkeys in the fall to yield sport and food. It has always been my practice to leave at least one old gobbler in each locality to assist the hens in reproduction. If every hunter would do this the problem of maintaining the turkey supply would be greatly solved.

The greatest of all causes for the decrease of wild turkeys lies in the killing of all the old gobblers in the spring. Some say the yearling gobblers will answer every purpose. I say they will not; they answer no purpose except to grow and make gobblers for the next year. The hens are all right—you need have no anxiety about them; they can take care of themselves; provided you leave them a male bird that gobbles, they will do the rest. Any suitable community can have all the wild turkeys it wants if it will obtain a few specimens and turn them into a small woodland about the beginning of spring, spreading grain of some sort for them daily. The turkeys will stay where the food is abundant and where there is a little brush in which to retire and rest.

Some hunters, or rather some writers, claim that the only time the wild turkey should be hunted is in the autumn and winter, and not in the spring. I have a different idea altogether, and claim that the turkey should not

14

be hunted before November, if then, December being better. By the first of November the young gobbler weighs from seven to nine pounds, the hens from four to seven pounds; in December and January the former weighs twelve pounds and the latter nine pounds. There you are. But suppose you did not hunt in the spring at all. How many old, long-bearded gobblers (the joy and delight above every sort of game on earth to the turkey hunter) would you bag in a year, or a lifetime? Possibly in ten years you would get one, unless by the merest accident, as they are rarely, if ever, found in company with the hens or young gobblers, but go in small bands by themselves, and from their exclusive and retiring nature it is a rare occasion when one is killed except in the gobbling season.

Take away the delight of the gobbling season from the turkey hunter, and the quest of the wild turkey would lose its fascination. In so expressing myself, I do not advise that the gobblers be persecuted and worried all through the gobbling season, from March to June, but believe they could be hunted for a limited time, namely, until the hens begin to lay and the gobblers to lose their fat—say until the first of April. Every old turkey hunter knows where to stop, and does it without limitation of law. Old gobblers are in their best condition until about the first of April, then they begin to lose flesh very rapidly. At this time hunting them should be abandoned altogether.

In my hunting trips after this bird I have covered most of the southern states, and have been interested to note that all the Indians I have met called the turkey "Furkee" or "Firkee"; the tribes I have hunted with include the Choctaws, Chickasaws, Creeks, Seminoles, and the Cherokees, who live east of the Mississippi River, and the Alabams, Conchattas, and Zunis of the west. Whether their name for the bird is a corruption of our turkey, or whether our word is a corruption of their "Furkee," I am not prepared to state. It may be that we get our name direct from the aboriginal Indians. All of the Indian tribes I have hunted with have legends concerning the turkey, and to certain of the Aztec tribes it was an object of worship. An old Zuni chief once told me a curious legend of his people concerning this bird, very similar to the story of the flood. It runs:

Ages ago, before man came to live on the earth, all birds, beasts, and fishes lived in harmony as one family, speaking the same language, and subsisting on sweet herbs and grass that grew in abundance all over the earth. Suddenly one day the sun ceased to shine, the sky became covered with heavy clouds, and rain began to fall. For a long time this continued, and neither the sun, moon, nor stars were seen. After a while the water got so deep that the birds, animals, and fishes had either to swim or fly in the air, as there was no land to stand on. Those that could not swim or fly were carried around on the backs of those that could, and this kept up until almost every living thing was almost starved. Then all the creatures held a meeting, and one from each kind was selected to go to heaven and ask the Great Spirit to send back the sun, moon, and stars and stop the rain. These journeyed a long way and at last found a great ladder running into the sky; they climbed up this ladder and found at the top a trapdoor leading into heaven, and on passing through the door, which was open, they saw the dwelling-place of man, and before the door were a boy and girl playing, and their playthings were the sun, moon, and stars belonging to the earth. As soon as the earth creatures saw the sun, moon, and stars, they rushed for them and, gathering them into a basket, took the children of man and hurried back to earth through the trapdoor. In their hurry to get away from the man whom they saw running after them, the trapdoor was slammed on the tail of the bear, cutting it off. The blood spattered over the lynx and trout, and since that time the bear has had no tail, and the lynx and trout are spotted. The buffalo fell down and hurt his back and has had a hump on it ever since. The sun, moon, and stars having been put back in their places, the rain stopped at once and the waters quickly dried up. On the first appearance of land, the turkey, who had been flying around all the time, lit, although warned not to do so by the other creatures. It at once began to sink in the mud, and its tail stuck to the mud so tight that it could hardly fly up, and when it did get away the end of its tail was covered with mud and is stained mud color to this day. The earth now having become dry and the children of man now lords of the earth, each creature was obliged to keep out of their way, so the fishes took to the waters using their tails to swim away from man, the birds took to their wings, and the animals took to their legs; and by these means the birds, beasts, and fishes have kept out of man's way ever since.

Before dealing with the wild turkeys as they are to-day, it will be well to make a short study of their prehistoric and historic standing; this has been ably done for me by Dr. R. W. Shufeldt of Washington, D. C., who has very kindly written for this work the next two chapters entitled "The Turkey Prehistoric," and "The Turkey Historic."

CHAPTER III
THE TURKEY PREHISTORIC

Probably no genus of birds in the American avifauna has received the amount of attention that has been bestowed upon the turkeys. Ever since the coming to the New World of the very first explorers, who landed in those parts where wild turkeys are to be found, there has been no cessation of verbal narratives, casual notices, and appearance of elegant literature relating to the members of this group. We have not far to seek for the reason for all this, inasmuch as a wild turkey is a very large and unusually handsome bird, commanding the attention of any one who sees it. Its habits, extraordinary behavior, and notes render it still more deserving of consideration; and to all this must be added the fact that wild turkeys are magnificent game birds; the hunting of them peculiarly attractive to the sportsman; while, finally, they are easily domesticated and therefore have a great commercial value everywhere.

The extensive literature on wild and domesticated turkeys is by no means confined to the English language, for we meet with many references to these fowls, together with accounts and descriptions of them, distributed through prints and publications of various kinds, not only in Latin, but in the Scandinavian languages as well as in French, German, Spanish, Italian, and doubtless in others of the Old World. Some of these accounts appeared as long ago as the early part of the sixteenth century, or perhaps even earlier; for it is known that Grijalva discovered Mexico in 1518, and Gomarra and Hernandez, whose writings appeared soon afterward, gave, among their descriptions of the products of that country, not only the wild turkey, but, in the case of the latter writer, referred to the wild as well as to the domesticated form, making the distinction between the two.

In order, however, to render our history of the wild turkeys in America as complete as possible, we must dip into the past many centuries prior to the discovery of the New World by those early navigators. We must go back to the time when it was questionable whether man existed upon this continent at all. In other words, we must examine and describe the material representing our extinct turkeys handed us by the paleontologists, or the fossilized remains of the prehistoric ancestors of the family, of which we have at hand a few fragments of the greatest value. These I shall refer to but briefly for several reasons. In the first place, their technical descriptions have already appeared in several widely known publications, and in the second, what I have here to say about them is in a popular work, and technical descriptions are not altogether in place. Finally, such material as we possess is very meagre in amount indeed, and such parts of it as would in any way interest the general reader can be referred to very briefly.

The fossil remains of a supposed extinct turkey, described by Marsh[1] as *Meleagris altus* from the Post-pliocene of New Jersey, is, from the literature and notices on the subject, now found to be but a synonym of the *Meleagris superba* of Cope from the Pleistocene of New Jersey. At the present writing I have before me the type specimen of *Meleagris altus* of Marsh, for which favor I am indebted to Dr. Charles Schuchert of the Peabody Museum of Yale University. My account of it will be published in another connection later on.

Some years after Professor Marsh had described this material as representing a species to which I have just said he gave the specific name of *altus*, it would appear that I did not fully concur in the propriety of doing so, as will be seen from a paper I published on the subject about fifteen years ago[2]. This will obviate the necessity of saying anything further in regard to *M. superba*.

So far as my knowledge carries me, this leaves but two other fossil wild turkeys of this country, both of which have been described by Professor Marsh and generally recognized. These are *Meleagris antiqua* in 1871, and *Meleagris celer* in 1872. My comments on both of these species will be found in the *American Naturalist* for July, 1897, on pages 648, 649.[3]

Plate I
Types: *M. antiqua*; *M. celer*. Marsh
Fig. 1. Anconal aspect of the distal extremity of the right humerus of "*Meleagris antiquus*" of Marsh. Fig. 2. Palmar aspect of the same specimen shown in Fig. 1. Fig. 3. Anterior aspect of the proximal moiety of the left tarso-metatarsus of *Meleagris celer* of

Marsh. Fig. 4. Posterior aspect of the same fragment of bone shown in Fig. 3. Fig. 5. Outer aspect of the same fragment of bone shown in Figs. 3 and 4. All figures natural size. Reproduced from photographs made *direct* from the specimens by Dr. R. W. Shufeldt.

It will be noted, then, that *Meleagris antiqua* of Marsh is practically represented by the *imperfect* distal extremity of a right humerus; and that *Meleagris celer* of the same paleontologist from the Pleistocene of New Jersey is said to be represented by the bones enumerated in a foregoing footnote. In this connection let it be borne in mind that, while I found fossil specimens of *Meleagris g. silvestris* in the bone caves of Tennessee, I found no remains of fossil turkeys in Oregon, from whence some classifiers of fossil birds state that *M. antiqua* came (A. O. U. Check-Listed, 1910, p. 388[4]).

On the 19th of April 1912, I communicated by letter with Dr. George F. Eaton, of the Museum of Yale University, in regard to the fossils described by Marsh of *M. antiqua* and *M. celer*, with the view of borrowing them for examination. Dr. Eaton, with great kindness, at once interested himself in the matter, and wrote me (April 20, 1912) that "We have a wise rule forbidding us to lend type material, but I shall be glad to ask Professor Schuchert to make an exception in your favor." In due time Prof. Charles Schuchert, then curator of the Geological Department of the Peabody Museum of Natural History of Yale University, wrote me on the subject (May 2, 1912), and with marked courtesy granted the request made of him by Dr. Eaton, and forwarded me the type specimen of Marsh of *M. antiqua* and *M. celer* by registered mail. They were received on the 3rd of May, 1912, and I made negatives of the two specimens on the same day. It affords me pleasure to thank both Professor Schuchert and Dr. Eaton here for the unusual privilege I enjoyed, through their assistance, in the loan of these specimens;[5] also Dr. James E. Benedict, Curator of Exhibits of the U. S. National Museum, and Dr. Charles W. Richmond of the Division of Birds of that institution, for their kindness in permitting me to examine and make notes upon a mounted skeleton of a wild turkey (*M. g. silvestris*) taken by Prof. S. F. Baird at Carlisle,

Penn., many years ago. Mr. Newton P. Scudder, librarian of the National Museum, likewise has my sincere thanks for his kindness in placing before me the many volumes on the history of the turkey I was obliged to consult in connection with the preparation of this chapter.

From what has already been set forth above, it is clear that Marsh's specimen (for he attached but scant importance to the *other fragments* with it), upon which he based "*Meleagris antiquus*" was not taken in Oregon, but in Colorado.[6] Both of these fossils I have very critically compared with the corresponding parts of the bones represented in each case in the skeleton of an adult wild turkey (*Meleagris g. silvestris*) in the collection of mounted bird skeletons in the U. S. National Museum.

Taking everything at my command into consideration as set forth above, as well as the extent of Professor Marsh's knowledge of the osteology of existing birds—not heretofore referred to—I am of the opinion, that in the case of his *Meleagris antiqua*, the material upon which it is based is altogether too fragmentary to pronounce, with anything like certainty, that it ever belonged to a turkey at all. In the first place, it is a very *imperfect* fragment (Plate 1, Figs. 1 and 2); in the second, it does not typically present the "characteristic portions" of that end of the humerus in a turkey, as Professor Marsh states it does. Thirdly, the distal end of the humerus is by no means a safe fragment of the skeleton of hardly any bird to judge from. Finally, it is questionable whether the genus *Meleagris* existed at all, as such, at the time the "Miocene clay deposits of northern Colorado" were deposited.

That this fragment may have belonged to the skeleton of some big gallinaceous fowl the size of an adult existing *Meleagris*—and long ago extinct—I in no way question; but that it was a *true turkey*, I very much doubt.

Still more uncertain is the fragment representing *Meleagris celer* of Marsh. (Plate 1, Figs. 3-5.) The tibia mentioned I have not seen, and of them Professor Marsh states that they only "probably belonged to the same individual" (see *antea*). As to this proximal moiety of the tarso-metatarsus, it is essentially different from the corresponding part of that bone in *Meleagris g. silvestris*. In it the *hypotarsus* is twice grooved, longitudinally; whereas in *M. g. silvestris* there is but a single median groove. In the latter bird there is a conspicuous osseous ridge extending far down the shaft of the bone, it being

21

continued from the internal, thickened border of the hypotarsus. This ridge is only *indicated* on the fossil bone, having either been broken off or never existed at all. In any event it is not present in the specimen. The general *facies* of the fossil is quite different from that part of the tarso-metatarsus in an existing wild turkey, and to me it does not seem to have come from the skeleton of the pelvic limb of a meleagrine fowl at all. It may have belonged to a bird of the galline group, not essentially a turkey; while on the other hand it may have been from the skeleton of some large wader, not necessarily related to either the true herons or storks. Some of the herons, for example, (*Ardea*) have "the hypotarsus of the tarso-metatarsus three-crested, graduated in size, the outer being the smaller; the tendinal grooves pass between them."[7] As just stated, the hypotarsus of the tarso-metatarsus in *Meleagris celer* of Marsh is three-crested, and the tendinal grooves pass between them. In *M. g. silvestris* this process is but two-crested and the median groove passes between them.

The *sternum* of the turkey, if we have it practically complete, is one of the most characteristic bones of the skeleton; but Professor Marsh had no such material to guide him when he pronounced upon his fossil turkeys. Had I made new species, based on the fragments of fossil long bones of all that I have had for examination, quite a numerous little extinct avifauna would have been created.

"It is often a positive detriment to science, in my opinion, to create new species of fossil birds upon the distal ends of long bones, and surely no assistance whatever to those who honestly endeavor to gain some idea of the avian species that really existed during prehistoric times."[8]

CHAPTER IV
THE TURKEY HISTORIC

Having disposed of such records as we have of the extinct ancestors of the American turkeys—the so-to-speak meleagrine records—we can now pass to what is, comparatively speaking, the modern history of these famous birds, although some of this history is already several centuries old.

We have seen in the foregoing chapter that all the described fossil species of turkeys have been restricted to the genus *Meleagris*, and this is likewise the case with the existing species and subspecies. Right here I may say that the word *Meleagris* is Greek as well as Latin, and means a guinea-fowl. This is due to the fact that when turkeys were first described and written about they were, by several authors of the early times, strangely mixed up with those African forms, and the two were not entirely disentangled for some time, as we shall see further on in this chapter. In modern ornithology, however, the generic name of *Meleagris* has been transferred from the guinea-fowls to the turkeys. These last, as they are classified in "The A. O. U. Check-List of the American Ornithologists' Union," which is the latest authoritative word upon the subject, stand as follows:

Family Meleagridæ. Turkeys.

Genus Meleagris Linnæus.

Meleagris Linnæus, Syst. Nat., ed. 10, 1, 1758, 156. Type, by subs, desig., *Meleagris gallopavo* Linnæus (Gray, 1840).
Meleagris gallopavo (Linnæus).
Range.—Eastern and south central United States, west to Arizona and south to the mountains of Oaxaca.

a. [Meleagris gallopavo gallopavo. Extralimital.]

b. Meleagris gallopavo silvestris Vieillot. Wild Turkey [310*a*].

Meleagris silvestris Vieillot Nouv., Dict. d'Hist. Nat., IX, 1817, 447.

Range.—Eastern United States from Nebraska, Kansas, western Oklahoma, and eastern Texas east to central Pennsylvania, and south to the

Gulf coast; formerly north to South Dakota, southern Ontario, and southern Maine.

c. Meleagris gallopavo merriami Nelson. Merriam's Turkey [310].

Meleagris gallopavo merriami Nelson, Auk, XVII, April, 1900, 120.
(47 miles southwest of Winslow, Arizona.)

Range.—Transition and Upper Sonoran zones in the mountains of southern Colorado, New Mexico, Arizona, western Texas, northern Sonora, and Chihuahua.

d. Meleagris gallopavo osceola Scott. Florida Turkey [310*b*].

Meleagris gallopavo osceola Scott, Auk, VII, Oct., 1890, 376. (Tarpon Springs, Florida.)

Range.—Southern Florida.

e. Meleagris gallopavo intermedia Sennett. Rio Grande Turkey [310*c*].

Meleagris gallopavo intermedia Sennett. Bull. U. S. Geol. & Geog. Surv. Terr., V, No. 3, Nov., 1879, 428. (Lomita, Texas.)

Range.—Middle northern Texas south to northeastern Coahuila, Nuevo Leon, and Tamaulipas.

The presenting of the above list here does away with giving, in the history of the wild turkeys, any of the very numerous changes that have taken place through the ages which led up to its adoption. The discussion of these changes, as a part of meleagrine history, would make an octavo volume of two hundred pages or more.

It may be said here, however, that the word *gallopavo* is from the Latin, *gallus* a cock, and *pavo* a peafowl, while the meanings of the several words *silvestris*, *merriami*, *osceola*, and *intermedia* are self-evident and require no definitions.

Audubon, who gives the breeding range of the wild turkey as extending "from Texas to Massachusetts and Vermont" (Vol. V., p. 56), says of them in his long account: "I have ascertained that some of these valuable birds are still to be found in the states of New York, Massachusetts, Vermont, and Maine. In the winter of 1832-33, I purchased a few fine males in the city of Boston"; and further, "At the time when I removed to Kentucky, rather more than a fourth of a century ago, turkeys were so abundant that the price of one in the market was not equal to that of a common barn-fowl now. I have seen them offered for the sum of three pence each, the birds weighing from ten to twelve pounds. A first-rate turkey, weighing from twenty-five to thirty pounds avoirdupois, was considered well sold when it brought a quarter of a dollar."[9]

From these remarks we may imagine how plentiful wild turkeys must have been on the North American continent, when Aristotle wrote his work "On Animals," over three hundred years before the birth of Christ, upward of twenty-three centuries ago! A good many changes can take place in the avifauna of a country in that time.

How these big, gallinaceous fowls ever got the name of "turkey" has long been a matter of dispute; and not a few ornithologists and writers of note in the 16th and 17th centuries erroneously conceived that the term had something to do either with the Turks or their country. But this idea has now been entirely abandoned, for it has become quite clear that, during the times mentioned, the turkey was strangely confused with the guinea-fowl, a bird to which the name turkey was originally applied.

Later on, both these birds became more abundant, as more of them were domesticated and reared in captivity, and the fact was gradually realized that they were entirely different species of fowls. During these times, the word turkey was finally applied only to the New World species, and the West African form was thereafter called "Guinea-fowl."[10] After the word turkey was more generally applied to the bird now universally so known, some believe that there was another reason as to how it came about, and this "possibly because of its reputed call-note," says Newton, "to be syllabled *turk, turk, turk*, whereby it may be almost said to have named itself." (Notes and Queries, ser. 6, III, pp. 23, 369.)[11]

Plate II

Fig. 6. Superior view of the skull of an old male wild turkey; lower jaw removed. No. 9695, Coll. U. S. National Museum. Fig. 7. Lower jaw or mandible of the skull shown in Fig. 6., seen from above. Fig. 8. Superior view of a skull of a wild turkey and probably a female. Lower jaw removed and shown in Fig. 9. No. 19684, Coll. U. S. National Museum. Fig. 9. Lower jaw of the skull shown in Fig. 8. Superior aspect. Fig. 10. Upper view of the skull of a wild Florida turkey (*Meleagris g. osceola*); lower jaw removed and not figured. Female. No. 18797, Coll. U. S. National Museum. All the figures in this plate are reproductions of photographs of the specimens made natural size by Dr. Shufeldt. Reduced about one-fourth.

So much for the origin of the name *turkey*; and when one comes to search through the literature devoted to this fowl to ascertain who first described the wild species, the opinion seems to be pretty general that this was done by Oviedo in the thirty-sixth chapter of his "Summario de la Natural Historia de las Indias," which it is stated appeared about the year 1527.

Professor Spencer F. Baird, apparently quoting Martin, says: "Oviedo speaks of the turkey as a kind of peacock abounding in New Spain, which had already in 1526 been transported in a domestic state to the West India Islands and the *Spanish Main*, where it was kept by the Christian colonists."[12]

In an elegant and comprehensive article on "The Wild Turkey," Bennett states: "Oviedo, whose Natural History of the Indies contains the earliest description extant of the bird, and whose acquaintance with the animal productions of the newly discovered countries was surprisingly extensive. He speaks of it as a kind of Peacock found in New Spain, of which a number had been transported to the islands of the Spanish Main, and domesticated in the houses of the Christian inhabitants. His description is exceedingly accurate, and proves that before the year 1526, when his work was published at Toledo, the turkey was already reduced to a state of

Domestication."[13]

Again, in a very elaborate and now thoroughly classical contribution, Pennant states: "The first precise description of these birds is given by Oviedo, who, in 1525, drew up a summary of his greater work, the History of the Indies, for the use of his monarch Charles V.[14] This learned man had visited the West Indies and its islands in person, and paid particular regard to the natural history. It appears from him, that the Turkey was in his days an inhabitant of the greater islands and of the mainland. He speaks of them as Peacocks; for being a new bird to him, he adopts that name from the resemblance he thought they bore to the former. 'But,' says he, 'the neck is bare of feathers, but covered with a skin which they change after their phantasie into diverse colours. They have a horn (in the Spanish Peçon corto) as it were on their front, and hairs on the breast.' (In Purchas, III, 995.) He describes other birds which he also calls Peacocks. They are of the gallinaceous genus, and known by the name of Curassao birds, the male of which is black, the female ferruginous."[15]

Dr. Coues, who has also written an article on the history of the wild turkey, which, by the way, is mainly composed of a lengthy quotation from the above cited article of Bennett's, says: "Linnæus, however, knew perfectly well that the turkey was American. He says distinctly: 'Habitat in America septentrionali,' and quotes as his first reference (after Fn. Soec. 198), the *Gallopavo sylvestris novæ angliæ*, or New England Wild Turkey of Ray. Brisson distinguished the two perfectly, giving an elaborate description, a copious synonomy, and a good figure of each; and from about this time it may be considered that the history of the two birds, so widely diverse, was finally disentangled, and the proper habitat ascribed to each." (Refers to first describers of the pintado and turkey.)[16]

So much for the earliest describers of the wild turkey, and I shall now pass on to the general history of the bird, and, through presenting what has been collected for us by the best authors on the subject, endeavor to show how, after the wild turkey was found in America by different navigators and explorers, it was brought, from time to time, to several of the countries of the Old World—chiefly Spain and Great Britain—from whence it probably was taken, upon different occasions, into other countries of the continent.

Wild turkeys have always been easy to capture, and we are aware of the fact that they are quite capable of crossing the Atlantic on shipboard in comfort and safety, landing in as good a condition—if properly cared for during the voyage—as when they left America. Josselyn (1672) in his *New England Rarities* (p. 9) has not a little to say on this point.

As already stated, the literature and bibliography of the turkey is quite sufficient to fill a good many volumes. Nothing of importance, however, has been added to it, gainsaying what we now have as a truthful account of the bird's introduction into Europe. Indeed Buffon (Ois, II, pp. 132-162), Broderip (*Zool. Recreat.* pp. 120-137), Pennant (*Arct. Zool.* pp. 291-300), and others, practically cleared up nearly all the points on this part of the turkey's history, making but a few statements that are not wholly reliable and worthy of acceptance. Pennant very properly ignored in his work Barrington's essay (*Miscellanies*, pp. 127-151) in which the latter attempted to prove that turkeys were known before America was discovered, and that they were shipped over there subsequently to its discovery!

I have already cited above Pennant's article in the Philosophical Transactions of the Royal Society of London (1781), and quoted from it to some extent. It is one of the standard writings on the wild turkey invariably referred to by all authors when writing on the history of that bird. As it is only accessible to the few, and so full of reliable information, I propose to give here, somewhat in full, those paragraphs in it having special reference to the historical side of our subject, and in doing so I retain the spelling and composition of the original production.

"Belon, ('Hist. des Oys.,' 248) the earliest of those writers," says Pennant, "who are of the opinion that these birds were natives of the old world, founds his notion on the description of the Guinea-fowl, the Meleagrides of Strabo, Athenæus, Pliny, and others of the ancients. I rest the refutation on the excellent account given by Athenæus, taken from Clytus Milesius, a disciple of Aristotle, which can suit no other than that fowl. 'They want,' says he, 'natural affection towards their young; their head is naked, and on the top is a hard round body like a peg or nail; from their cheeks hangs a

28

red piece of flesh like a beard. It has no wattles like the common poultry. The feathers are black, spotted with white. They have no spurs; and both sexes are so alike as not to be distinguished by the sight.' Varro (Lib. III. c. 9.) and Pliny (Lib. X. c. 26) take notice of the spotted plumage and the gibbous substance on the head. Athenæus is more minute, and contradicts every character of the Turkey, whose females are remarkable for their natural affection, and differ materially in form from the males, whose heads are destitute of the callous substance, and whose heels (in the males) are armed with spurs."

"Aldrovandus, who died in 1605, draws his arguments from the same source as Belon; I therefore pass him by, and take notice of the greatest of our naturalists Gesner (Av. 481.), who falls into a mistake of another kind, and wishes the Turkey to be thought a native of India. He quotes Ælian for that purpose, who tells us, 'That in India are very large poultry not with combs, but with various coloured crests interwoven like flowers, with broad tails either bending or displayed in a circular form, which they draw along the ground as peacocks do when they do not erect them; and that the feathers are partly of a gold colour, partly blue, and of an emerald colour.' (De Anim. lib. XVI, c. 2.).

"This in all probability was the same bird with the Peacock Pheasant of Mr. Edwards, *Le Baron de Tibet* of M. Brisson, and the *Pavo bicalcaratus* of Linnæus. I have seen this bird living. It has a crest, but not so conspicuous as that described by Ælian; but it has not those striking colours in form of eyes, neither does it erect its tail like the Peacock (Edw. II. 67.), but trails it like the Pheasant. The *Catreus* of Strabo (Lib. XV. p. 1046) seems to be the same bird. He describes it as uncommonly beautiful and spotted, and very like a Peacock. The former author (De Anim. lib. XVII, c. 23.) gives more minute account of this species, and under the same name. He borrows it from Clitarchus, an attendant of Alexander the Great in all his conquests. It is evident from his description that it was of this kind; and it is likewise probable that it was the same with his large Indian poultry before cited. He celebrates it also for its fine note; but allowance must be made for the credulity of Ælian.

"The *Catreus*, or Peacock Pheasant, is a native of Tibet, and in all probability of the north of India, where Clitarchus might have observed it; for the march of Alexander was through that part which borders on Tibet, and is now known by the name of Penj-ab or five rivers."

"I shall now collect from authors the several parts of the world where Turkies are unknown in the state of nature. Europe has no share in the question; it being generally agreed that they are exotic in respect to that continent."

"Neither are they found in any part of Asia Minor, or the Asiatic Turkey, notwithstanding ignorance of their true origin first caused them to be named from that empire. About Aleppo, capital of Syria, they are only met with, domesticated like other poultry. (Russel, 63). In Armenia they are unknown, as well as in Persia; having been brought from Venice by some Armenian merchants into that empire (Tavernier, 145), where they are still so scarce as to be preserved among other rare fowls in the royal menagery" (Bell's Travels, I. 128).

"Du Halde acquaints us that they are not natives of China; but were introduced there from other countries. He errs from misinformation in saying that they are common in India."

"I will not quote Gemelli Careri, to prove that they are not found in the Philippine Islands, because that gentleman with his pen traveled round the world in his easy chair, during a very long indisposition and confinement, (Sir James Porter's Obs. Turkey, I, 1, 321), in his native country."

"But Dampier bears witness that none are found in Mindanao" (Barbot in Churchill's Coll., V. 29).

"The hot climate of Africa barely suffers these birds to exist in that vast continent, except under the care of mankind. Very few are found in Guinea, except in the hands of the Europeans, the negroes declining to breed any on account of the great heats (Bosman, 229). Prosper Alpinus satisfies us they are not found either in Nubia or in Egypt. He describes the Meleagrides of the ancients, and only proves that the Guinea hens were brought out of Nubia, and sold at a great price at Cairo (Hist. Nat. Ægypti. I, 201); but is totally silent about the turkey of the moderns."

"Let me in this place observe that the Guinea hens have long been imported into Britain. They were cultivated in our farm-yards; for I discover in 1277, in the Grainge of Clifton, in the parish of Ambrosden in Buckinghamshire, among other articles, six *Mutilones* and six *Africanæ fœminæ* (Kennett's Parochial Antiq. 287), for this fowl was familiarly known by the names of Afra Avis and Gallina Africana and Numida. It was introduced into Italy from Africa, and from Rome into our country. They were neglected here by reason of their tenderness and difficulty of rearing. We do not find them in the bills of fare of our ancient feasts (neither in that of George Nevil nor among the delicacies mentioned in the Northumberland household book begun in the beginning of the reign of Henry VIII); neither do we find the turkey; which last argument amounts almost to a certainty, that such a hardy and princely bird had not found its way to us. The other likewise was then known by its classical name; for that judicious writer Doctor Caius describes in the beginning of the reign of Elizabeth, the Guinea-fowl, for the benefit of his friend Gesner, under the name of Meleagris, bestowed on it by Aristotle" (CAII Opusc. 13. Hist. An., lib. VI. c. 2).

"Having denied, on the very best authorities, that the Turkey ever existed as a native of the old world, I must now bring my proofs of its being only a native of the new, and of the period in which it first made its appearance in Europe."

"The next who speaks of them as natives of the mainland of the warmer parts of America is Francusco Fernandez, sent there by Philip II, to whom he was physician. This naturalist observed them in Mexico. We find by him that the name of the male was Huexolotl, of the female Cihuatotolin. He gives them the title of Gallus Indicus and Gallo Pavo. The Indians, as well as the Spaniards, domesticated these useful birds. He speaks of the size by comparison, saying that the wild were twice the magnitude of the tame; and that they were shot with arrows or guns (Hist. Av. Nov. Hisp. 27). I cannot learn the time when Fernandez wrote. It must be between the years 1555 and 1598, the period of Philip's reign."

"Pedro de Ciesa mentions Turkies on the Isthmus of Darien (Seventeen Years Travels, 20). Lery, a Portuguese author, asserts that they are found in Brazil, and gives them an Indian name (In De Laet's Descr. des Indes, 491); but since I can discover no traces of them in that diligent and excellent naturalist Marcgrave, who resided long in that country, I must deny my assent. But the former is confirmed by that able and honest navigator Dampier, who saw them frequently, as well wild as tame, in the province of Yucatan (Voyages, Vol II, part II, pp. 65, 85, 114), now reckoned part of the Kingdom of Mexico."

"In North America they were observed by the very first discoverers. When Rene de Landonniere, patronized by Admiral Coligni, attempted to form a settlement near where Charlestown now stands, he met with them on his first landing in 1564, and by his historian has represented them with great fidelity in the fifth plate of the recital of his voyage (Debry): from his time the witnesses to their being natives of the continent are innumerable. They have been seen in flocks of hundreds in all parts from Louisiana even to Canada; but at this time are extremely rare in a wild state, except in the more distant parts, where they are still found in vast abundance."

"It was from Mexico or Yucatan that they were first introduced into Europe; for it is certain that they were imported into England as early as the year 1524, the 15th of Henry VIII. (Baker's Chr. Anderson's Dict., Com. 1, 354. Hackluyt, II, 165, makes their introduction about the year 1532. Barnaby Googe, one of our early writers on Husbandry, says they were not seen here before 1530. He highly commends a Lady Hales of Kent for her excellent management of these fowl, p. 166.)

"We probably received them from Spain, with which we had great intercourse till about that time. They were most successfully cultivated in our Kingdom from that period; insomuch that they grew common in every farm-yard, and became even a dish in our rural feasts by the year 1585; for we may certainly depend on the word of old Tusser in his Account of the Christmas Husbandrie Fare." (Five Hundred Points of good Husbandrie, p. 57.)

"Beefe, Mutton, and Porke, shredpiece of the best, Pig, Veale, Goose, and Capon, and Turkie well drest, Cheese, Apples and Nuts, jolie carols to heare, As then in the countrie, is counted good cheare."

"But at this very time they were so rare in France, that we are told, that the very first which was eaten in that Kingdom appeared at the nuptial feast of Charles IX. in 1570 (Anderson's Dict. Com. 1, 410)."[17]

32

Plate III

Fig. II. Left lateral view of the skull of an old male wild turkey (*Meleagris gallopavo*). See Plate II, Fig. 6, No. 9695, Coll. U. S. National Museum. Photo natural size by Dr. Shufeldt. *pmx*, premaxillary; *n*, nasal bone; *l*, lacrymal bone; *eth*, ethmoid; *p*, parietal; *so*, supraoccipital; *pl*, palatine; *ju*, jugal; *ty*, tympanic; *q*, quadrate; *a*, angular of lower jaw; *d*, dentary. There are many more bones in the skull than those indicated, while the latter serve to invite attention to the principal ones as landmarks.

A little later on Bartram in his travels in the South published some notes on the wild turkey [now *M. g. osceola*] as he found them in Florida during the latter part of the eighteenth century. The original edition of his book, which I have not seen, appeared in 1791. I have, however, examined the edition of 1793, wherein on page 14 he says: "Our turkey of America is a very different species from the Meleagris of Asia and Europe; they are nearly thrice their size and weight. I have seen several that have weighed between twenty and thirty pounds, and some have been killed that have weighed near forty."

And further on in the same work he adds [Florida, p. 81]: "Having rested very well during the night, I was awakened in the morning early by the cheering converse of the wild turkey-cocks (Meleagris occidentalis) saluting each other from the sun-brightened tops of the lofty Cupressus disticha and Magnolia grandiflora. They begin at early dawn and continue till sunrise, from March to the last of April. The high forests ring with the noise, like the crowing of the domestic cock, of these social sentinels; the watchword being caught and repeated, from one to another, for hundreds of miles around, insomuch that the whole country is for an hour or more in a universal shout. A little after sunrise, their crowing gradually ceases, they quit then their high lodging places, and alight on the earth, where, expanding their silver-bordered train, they strut and dance round about the coy female, while the deep forests seem to tremble with their shrill noise."[18]

Another of the early writers (1806), who paid some attention to the history and distribution of the wild turkeys was Barton. I find the following having reference to some of his observations, viz.: "A memoir has been read before the American Philosophical Society in which the author has shown that at least two distinct species of Meleagris, or turkey, are known within the limits of North America. These are the *Meleagris gallopavo*, or Common Domesticated Turkey, which was wholly unknown in the countries of the Old World before the discovery of America; and the Common Wild Turkey of the United States, to which the author of the memoir has given the name *Meleagris Palawa*—one of its Indian names.

"The same author has rendered it very probable that this latter species was *domesticated* by *some* of the Indian tribes living within the *present* limits of the United States, before these tribes had been visited by the Europeans. It is certain, however, that the turkey was not domesticated by the *generality* of the tribes, within the limits just mentioned, until *after* the Europeans had taken possession of the countries of North America."[19]

Nine or ten years after Barton wrote, De Witt Clinton, who was a candidate for President of the United States in 1812, and a son of James Clinton, was one of the writers of that time on the wild turkey. He pointed out how birds, the turkey included, change their plumage after domestication, and, after giving what he knew of the introduction of the turkey into Spain from America and the West Indies, he adds: "From the Spanish turkey, which was thus spread over Europe, we have obtained our domestic one. The wild turkey has been frequently tamed, and his offspring is of a large size." (p. 126.)[20]

Nearly a quarter of a century after Clinton's article appeared, the *anatomy* of the wild turkey began to attract some attention. Among the first articles to appear on this part of the subject was one by the late Sir Richard Owen, who, apparently taking the similarity of the vernacular names into account, made anatomical comparisons of the organs of smell in the turkey and the turkey buzzard. Naturally, he found them very different,—quite as different, perhaps, as are the olfactory organs of an owl and an ostrich, which I, for one, would not undertake to make a comparison of for publication, simply for the fact that in both these birds their vernacular name begins with the letter o.[21]

Even twenty years after this paper appeared there were those who still entertained doubts as to the origin of the domesticated turkeys, and believed that they had nothing to do with the wild forms. Among the doubters, no one was more prominent than Le Conte, who published the following as his opinion at the time, stating: "The conviction that these two birds were really distinct species has long existed in my mind. More than fifty years ago, when I first saw a Wild Turkey, I was led to conclude that one never could have been produced from the other." [Bases it on differences of external characters] (p. 179), adding toward the close of his article: "I defy anyone to show a Turkey, even of the first generation, produced from a pair hatched from the eggs of a wild hen," etc. "I repeat, contrary to the assertions of many others, that no one has ever succeeded in domesticating our Wild Turkey," etc. "Thoroughly believe that the tame and wild bird are different species, and the latter not the ancestor of the tame one." (p. 181.)[22]

During the year 1856, the papers Gould published on the wild turkeys attracted considerable attention, and they have been widely quoted since. In one of his first papers on the subject he quotes from Martin the same paragraph which Baird quoted in his article in the Report of the Commissioner of Agriculture (1866 *antea*), while Baird in his article misquotes Gould by saying that the turkey was introduced into England in 1541; whereas Gould states the introduction took place in 1524.[23]

Before passing to the more recent literature on these birds, and what I will have to say further on about their comparative osteology and their eggs, it will be as well to reproduce here a few more statements made by Bennett, whose work, "The Gardens and Menagerie of the Zoölogical Society Delineated," I have already quoted.[24]

Bennett was also of the opinion that "Daines Barrington was the last writer of any note who denied the American origin of the turkey, and he seems to have been actuated more by a love of paradox than by any conviction of the truth of his theory. Since the publication of his Miscellanies, in 1781, the knowledge that has been obtained of the existence of large flocks of turkeys, perfectly wild, clothed in their natural plumage, and displaying their native habits, spread over a large portion of North America, together with the certainty of their non-existence in a similar state in any other part of the globe, have been admitted on all hands to be decisive of the question." (p. 210).

I have already cited the evidence above to prove that it was Oviedo who first published an accurate description of the wild turkey,—his work being published at Toledo in about the year 1526, at which time the turkey had already become domesticated. In other words, it was the Spaniards who first reduced the bird to a state of domestication, and very soon thereafter it was introduced into England. Spain and England were the great maritime nations of those times, and this fact will amply account for the early introduction of the bird into the latter country. Singularly enough, however, we have no account of any kind whatever through which we can trace the exact time when this took place. As others have suggested, it is just possible that it may have been Cabot, the explorer of the then recently discovered coasts of America, who first transported wild turkeys into England. Baker quotes the popular rhyme in his Chronicle:

"Turkeys, carps, hoppes, picarel and beer, Came into England all in one year,"

that is, about 1524, or the 15th of the reign of Henry VIII.[25]

What was said by the German author Heresbach was translated by a writer on agricultural subjects, Barnaby Googe, who published it in his work. This appeared in the year 1614, and he refers to "those outlandish birds called Ginny-Cocks and Turkey-Cocks," stating that "before the yeare of our Lord 1530 they were not seene with us!"

Further, Bennett points out that "A more positive authority is Hakluyt, who in certain instructions given by him to a friend at Constantinople, bearing date of 1582, mentions, among other valuable things introduced into England from foreign parts, 'Turkey-Cocks and hennes' as having been brought in 'about fifty years past.' We may therefore fairly

36

conclude that they became known in this country about the year 1530."[26]

Guinea-fowls were extremely rare in England throughout the sixteenth century, while tame turkeys became very abundant there, forming by no means an expensive dish at festivals,—the first were obtained from the Levant, while the latter were to be found in poultry yards nearly everywhere. In one of the Constitutions of Archbishop Cranmer it was ordered that of fowls as large as swans, cranes, and turkey-cocks, "there should be but one in a dish."[27]

When in 1555 the serjeants-at-law were created, they provided for their inauguration dinner two turkeys and four turkey chicks at a cost each of only four shillings, swans and cranes being ten, and half a crown each for capons. At this rate, turkeys could not have been so very scarce in those parts.[28] "Indeed they had become so plentiful in 1573," continues Bennett, "that honest Tusser, in his 'Five Hundred Points of Good Husbandrie,'" enumerates them among the usual Christmas fare at a farmer's table, and speaks of them as "ill neighbors" both to "peason" and to hops. (pp. 212, 213.)

"A Frenchman named Pierre Gilles has the credit of having first described the turkey in this quarter of the globe, in his additions to a Latin translation of Ælian, published by him in 1535. His description is so true to nature as to have been almost wholly relied on by every subsequent writer down to Willoughby. He speaks of it as a bird that he has seen; and he had not then been further from his native country than Venice; and states it to have been brought from the New World.

"That turkeys were known in France at this period is further proved by a passage in Champier's 'Treatise de Re Cibaria,' published in 1560, and said to have been written thirty years before. This author also speaks of them as having been brought but a few years back from the newly discovered Indian islands. From this time forward their origin seems to have been entirely forgotten, and for the next two centuries we meet with little else in the writings of ornithologists concerning them than an accumulation of citations from the ancients, which bear no manner of relation to them. In the year 1566 a present of twelve turkeys was thought not unworthy of being offered by the municipality of Amiens to their king, at whose marriage, in

1570, Anderson states in his History of Commerce, but we know not on what authority, they were first eaten in France. Heresbach, as we have seen, asserts that they were introduced into Germany about 1530; and that a sumptuary law made at Venice in 1557, quoted by Zanoni, particularizes the tables at which they were permitted to be served.

"So ungrateful are mankind for the most important benefits that not even a traditionary vestige remains of the men by whom, or the country from whence, this most useful bird was introduced into any European states. Little therefore is gained from its early history beyond the mere proof of the rapidity with which the process of domestication may sometimes be effected." (pp. 213, 214.)

Some ten or more years ago, at a time when I was the natural history editor of *Shooting and Fishing*, in New York City, I published a number of criticisms and original articles upon turkeys, both the wild and domesticated forms.[29]

About twelve years ago, Mr. Nelson contributed a very valuable article on wild turkeys, portions of which are eminently worthy of the space here required to quote them.[30] He says among other things in this article that "All recent ornithologists have considered the wild turkey of Mexico and the southwestern United States (aside from *M. gallopavo intermedia*) as the ancestor of the domesticated bird. This idea is certainly erroneous, as is shown by the series of specimens now in the collection of the Biological Survey. When the Spaniards first entered Mexico they landed near the present city of Vera Cruz and made their way thence to the City of Mexico.

Plate IV
Fig. 12. Superior view of the cranium of a large male tame turkey, with right nasal bone (*n*) attached *in situ*. Specimen in Dr. Shufeldt's private collection. Fig. 13. Left lateral view of the skull of a female turkey, probably a wild one. No. 19684, Coll. U. S. National Museum. (See Fig. 8, Pl. II.) *e*, bony entrance to ear. Compare contour line of cranium with Fig. 14. Fig. 14. Left lateral view of the cranium of a tame turkey; male. Dr. Shufeldt's private collection. Fig. 15. Direct

posterior view of the cranium of a tame turkey, probably a female. *pf,* postfrontal. Specimen in Dr. Shufeldt's collection. Fig. 16. Skull of a wild Florida turkey, seen from below (*M. g. osceola*). (See Fig. 10, Pl. II.) Bones named in Fig. 18. Photo natural size by Dr. Shufeldt and considerably reduced.

"At this time they found domesticated turkeys among the Indians of that region, and within a few years the birds were introduced into Spain.[31]

"The part of the country occupied by the Spanish during the first few years of the conquest in which wild turkeys occur is the eastern slope of the Cordillera in Vera Cruz, and there is every reason to suppose that this must have been the original home of the birds domesticated by the natives of that region.

"Gould's description of the type of *M. mexicana* is not sufficiently detailed to determine the exact character of this bird, but fortunately the type was figured in Elliot's "Birds of North America.""... In addition Gould's type apparently served for the description of the adult male *M. gallopavo* in the 'Catalogue of Birds Brit. Mus.' (xxii, p. 387), and an adult female is described in the same volume from Ciudad Ranch Durango.... Thus it will become necessary to treat *M. gallopavo* and *M. mexicana* as at least subspecifically distinct. Whatever may be the relationship of *M. mexicana* to *M. gallopavo*, the *M. g. merriami* is easily separable from *M. g. mexicana* of the Sierra Madre of western Mexico, from Chihuahua to Colima. Birds from northern Chihuahua are intermediate."

In this article Mr. Nelson names *M. g. merriami* and gives full descriptions of the adult male and female in winter plumage.

What has thus far been presented above on the first discovery of the American wild turkeys, their natural history in the New World, their introduction into Spain, England, France, and elsewhere, is practically all we have on this part of our subject up to date. What I have given is from the very best ornithological and other authorities. Domesticated turkeys are now found in nearly all parts of the world, while in only a very few instances has any record been kept of the different times of their introduction. With the view of accumulating such data, one would have to search the histories of all the countries of all the civilized and semi-civilized peoples of the world, which would be the labor of almost a man's entire lifetime, and in only too many instances his search would be in vain, for the several records of the times of introducing these birds were not made.

Apart from the description of the wild turkeys, there is still a very large literature devoted to the domesticated forms of turkeys as they occur in this country and abroad, as well as descriptions of their eggs. I have gone over a large part of this literature, but shall be able to use only a small, though nevertheless essential, part of it here. This I shall complete with an account of *turkey eggs*, which will be presented quite apart from anything to do with their nests, nesting habits, and much else which will be fully treated in other chapters of this book. In some works we meet with the literature of all these subjects together, others have only a part, while still others are confined to one thing, as the eggs.[32] Darwin in his works paid considerable attention to the wild and tame turkeys. He states that "Professor Baird believes (as quoted in Tegetmeier's 'Poultry Book,' 1866, p. 269) that our turkeys are descended from a West Indian species, now extinct. But besides the improbability of a bird having long ago become extinct in these large and luxuriant islands, it appears, as we shall presently see, that the turkey degenerates in India, and this fact indicates that this was not aboriginally an inhabitant of the lowlands of the tropics.

"F. Michaux," he further points out, "suspected in 1802 that the common domestic turkey was not descended from the United States species alone, but was likewise from a southern form, and he went so far as to believe that English and French turkeys differed from having different proportions of the blood of the two parent-forms.[33]

"English turkeys are smaller than either wild form. They have not varied in any great degree; but there are some breeds which can be distinguished—as Norfolks, Suffolks, Whites, and Copper-Coloured (or Cambridge), all of which, if precluded from crossing with other breeds, propagate their kind truly. Of these kinds, the most distinct is the small, hardy, dull-black Norfolk turkey, of which the chickens are black, with occasionally white patches about the head. The other breeds scarcely differ except in colour, and their chickens are generally mottled all over with brownish-grey.[34]

"In Holland there was formerly, according to Temminick, a beautiful buff-yellow breed, furnished with an ample white topknot. Mr. Wilmot has described a white turkey-cock with a crest formed of 'feathers about four inches long, with bare quills, and a tuft of soft down growing at the end.'[35] Many of the young birds whilst young inherited this kind of crest, but afterwards it either fell off or was pecked out by the other birds. This is an interesting case, as with care a new breed might probably have been formed; and a topknot of this nature would have been, to a certain extent, analogous to that borne by the males in several allied genera, such as *Euplocomus*, *Lophophorus*, and *Pavo*."[36]

Darwin has further pointed out that "The tuft of hair on the breast of the wild turkey-cock cannot be of any use, and it is doubtful whether it can be ornamental in the eyes of the female birds; indeed, had the tuft appeared under domestication, it would have been called a monstrosity.

"The naked skin on the head of a vulture is generally considered as a direct adaptation for wallowing in putridity; and so it may be, or it may possibly be due to the direct action of putrid matter; but we should be very cautious in drawing any such inference, when we see that the skin on the head of the clean-feeding male turkey is likewise naked."[37]

Plate V
Fig. 17. Left lateral view of the skull, including lower jaw, of a wild turkey; probably a female. No. 19684, Coll. U. S. National Museum. (See Fig. 8, Pl. II, and Fig. 13.) *ena*, external narial aperture. Fig. 18. Skull of wild Florida turkey. (See Fig. 16.) *pmx*, premaxillary; *l*, lacrymal; *pt*, pterygoids; *q*, quadrate; *c*, occipital condyle; *mxp*, maxillo-palatine; *pl*, palatines. Fig. 19. Skeleton of the left foot of a wild turkey (female?) No. 19684, Coll. U. S. National Museum. Several views of the skull of this individual are given above. The shortest toe is

the hind toe or hallux, and has a claw and a joint; then there are 3, 4, and 5 phalangeal joints to the second, third, and fourth toes respectively—that is in the inner, middle, and outer one. This count includes the distal or claw joints (ungual joints). All three figures photo natural size by Dr. Shufeldt and considerably reduced in reproduction.

Newton has pointed out that the topknotted turkeys were figured by Albin in 1738, and that it "has been suggested with some appearance of probability that the Norfolk breed may be descended from the northern form, *Meleagris gallopavo* or *americana*, while the Cambridgeshire breed may spring from the southern form the *M. mexicana* of Gould (P. Z. S. 1856, p. 61), which indeed it very much resembles, especially in having its tail-coverts and quills tipped with white or light ochreous—points that recent North American ornithologists rely upon as distinctive of this form. If this supposition be true, there would be reason to believe in the double introduction of the bird into England at least, as already hinted, but positive information is almost wholly wanting." (*Ibid.*, p. 996.).

It is an interesting fact that the males of both the wild and tame forms of turkeys frequently lack spurs;[38] and Henshaw has pointed out that in the case of *M. g. merriami* "A few of the gobblers had spurs; in one instance these took the form of a blunt, rounded knob half an inch long. In others, however, it was much reduced, and in others still the spur was wanting; though my impression is that all the old males had this weapon."[39]

One of the best articles which have been contributed to the present part of our subject, appeared several years ago from the pen of that very excellent naturalist, the late Judge Caton of Chicago. This contribution is rather a long one, and I shall only select such paragraphs from it as are of special value in the present connection.[40]

It is a well-known fact that the author of this work made a long series of observations on wild turkeys which he kept in confinement. He raised many from the eggs of the wild turkey taken in nature and hatched out by the common hen on his own preserves. At one time he had as many as sixty such birds, and he lost no opportunity to study their habits. They were of the pure stock with all their characters as in the wild form. These turkeys became very tame when thus raised from the eggs of the wild birds, and they did not deteriorate, either in size or in their power of reproduction. "This magnificent game bird," says Caton, "was never a native of the Pacific Coast. I have at various times sent in all about forty to California, in the hope that it may be acclimatized in the forests. Their numerous enemies have thus far prevented success in this direction, but they have done reasonably well in domestication, and Captain Rodgers of the United States Coast Survey has met with remarkable success in hybridizing them with the domestic bronze turkey. Last spring I sent some which were placed on Santa Clara Island, off Santa Barbara. They remained contentedly about the ranch building and, as I am informed, raised three broods of young which are doing well. As there is nothing on the island more dangerous to them than a very small species of fox, we may well hope that they will in a few years stock the whole island, which is many miles in extent. As the island is uninhabited except by the shepherds who tend the immense flocks of sheep there, they will soon revert to the wild state, when I have no doubt they will resume markings as constant as is observed in the wild bird here, but I shall be disappointed if the changed condition of life does not produce a change of color or in the shades of color, which would induce one unacquainted with their history to pronounce them specifically different from their wild ancestors here. Results will be watched with interest.

"My experiments in crossing the wild with the tame have been eminently successful." (Followed by a long account, p. 329.)

"My experiments establish first that the turkey may be domesticated, and that each succeeding generation bred in domestication loses something of the wild disposition of its ancestors.

"Second, that the wild turkey bred in domestication changes its form and the color of its plumage and of its legs, each succeeding generation degenerating more and more from these brilliant colors which are so constant on the wild turkey of the forest, so that it is simply a question of time—and indeed a very short time—when they will lose all of their native wildness and become clothed in all the varied colors of the common domestic turkey; in fact be like our domestic turkey,—yes, be our domestic turkey.

"Third, that the wild turkey and the domestic turkey as freely interbred as either does with its own variety, showing not the least sexual aversion always observed between animals of different species of the same genus, and that the hybrid progeny is as vigorous, as robust, and fertile as was either parent.

"It must be already apparent that I, at least, have no doubt that our common domestic turkey is a direct descendant of the wild turkey of our forests, and that therefore there is no specific difference between them. If such marked changes in the wild turkey occur by only ten years of domestication, all directly tending to the form, habits, and colorings of the domestic turkey,—in all things which distinguish the domestic from the wild turkey,—what might we not expect from fifty or a hundred years of domestication? I know that the best ornithological authority at the present time declares them to be of a different species, but I submit that this is a question which should be reconsidered in the light of indisputable facts which were not admitted or established at the time such decision was made.

"There has always been diffused among the domestic turkeys of the frontiers more or less of the blood of the wild turkey of the neighboring forests, and as the wild turkey has been driven back by the settlement of the country, the domestic turkey has gradually lost the markings which told of the presence of the wild; though judicious breeding has preserved and rendered more or less constant some of this evidence in what is called the domestic bronze turkey, as the red leg and the tawny shade dashed upon the white terminals of the tail feathers and the tail-coverts, the better should the stock be considered, because it is the more like its wild ancestor.

"That the domestic turkey in its neighborhood may be descended from or largely interbred with the wild turkey of New Mexico, which in its wild state more resembles the common domestic turkey than our wild turkey does, may unquestionably be true, and it may be also that the wild turkey there has a large infusion of the tame blood, for it is known that not only our domestic turkey, but even our barnyard fowls, relapse to the wild state in a single generation when they are reared in the woods and entirely away from the influence of man, gradually assuming uniform and constant colorings. But I will not discuss the question whether the Mexican wild turkey is of a different species from ours or merely a variety of the same species, only with differences in color which have arisen from accidental causes, and certainly I will not question that the Mexican turkey is the parent of many domestic turkeys, but I cannot resist the conclusion that our wild turkey is the progenitor of our domestic turkey."

We have now come to where we can study the eggs of these birds, and in the same article I have just quoted so extensively from, Judge Caton says on page 324 of it, "The eggs of the wild turkey vary much in coloring and somewhat in form, but in general are so like those of the tame turkey that no one can select one from the other. The ground color is white, over which are scattered reddish-brown specks. These differ in shades of color, but much more in numbers. I have seen some on which scarcely any specks could be detected, while others were profusely covered with specks, all laid by the same hen in the same nest. The turkey eggs are more pointed than those of the goose or the barnyard fowl, and are much smaller in proportion to the size of the bird."

This, in the main, is a fair description of the eggs of *Meleagris*, while at the same time it may be said that the ground color is not always "white," nor the markings exactly what might be denominated "specks."

Turkey eggs of all kinds, laid by hens of the wild as well as by those of the domesticated birds, have been described and figured in a great many popular and technically scientific books and other works, in this country as well as abroad. A large part of this literature I have examined, but I soon became convinced of the fact that *no general description* would begin to stand for the different kinds of eggs that turkeys lay. They not only differ in size, form, and markings, but in ground colors, numbers to the clutch, and some other particulars. Then it is true that no wild turkey hen, of any of the known subspecies or species of this country, has ever laid an egg but what some hen of the domestic breeds somewhere has not laid one practically exactly like it in all particulars. In other words, the eggs of our various breeds of tame turkeys are like the eggs of the several forms of the wild bird, that is, the subspecies known to science in the United States avifauna. Therefore I have not thought it necessary to present here any descriptions of the eggs of the tame turkeys or reproductions of photographs of the same.

Among the most beautiful of the wild turkey eggs published are those which appear in Major Bendire's work. They were drawn and painted by Mr. John L. Ridgway of the United States Geological Survey.[41] These very eggs I have not only examined, studied and compared, but, thanks to Dr. Richmond of the Division of Birds of the Museum, and to Mr. J. H. Riley, his assistant, I had such specimens as I needed loaned me from the general collection of the Museum, in that I might photograph them for use in the present connection. Dr. Richmond did me a special kindness in selecting for my study the four eggs here reproduced from my photograph of them in Plate VI. These are all of *M. g. silvestris*.

Of these, figures 20 and 21 are from the same clutch, and doubtless laid by the same bird. (Nos. 30014, 30014.) They were collected by J. H. Riley at Falls Church, Va. Figure 20 is an egg measuring 66 mm. x 45 mm., the color being a pale buffy-brown, finely and nearly evenly speckled all over with umber-brown, with very minute specks to dots measuring a millimetre in diameter. The finest speckling, with no larger spots, is at the greater end (butt) for a third of the egg.

Plate VI

Eggs of wild turkey (*M. g. silvestris*)

Names and descriptions given in the text. All the specimens photo natural size by Dr. Shufeldt and somewhat reduced in reproduction. Fig. 20. Upper left-hand one. Fig. 21. Upper right-hand one. Fig. 22. Lower left-hand one. Fig. 23. Lower right-hand one.

Figure 21 measures 63 mm. x 45 mm., the ground color being a pale cream, speckled somewhat thickly and uniformly all over with fine specks of light brown and lavender, with larger spots and ocellated marks of lavender moderately abundant over the middle and the apical thirds, with none about the larger end or remaining third. Figure 22 (Plate VI) is No. 31185 of the collection of the U. S. National Museum (ex Ralph Coll.); it was collected at Bridgeport, Michigan, by Allan Herbert (376, 4700, '77) and measures 68 x 46. It is of a rather deep buffy-brown or ochre, very thickly and quite uniformly speckled all over with more or less minute specks of dark brown.

Figure 23 was collected by H. R. Caldwell (91310), the locality being unrecorded (Coll. U. S. Nat. Museum, No. 32407), and measures 63 x 48. It is of a pale buffy-brown or pale *café au lait* color, quite thickly speckled all over with fine dots and specks of light brown. Some few of the specks are of noticeably larger size, and these are confined to the middle and apical thirds. Speckling of the butt or big end extremely fine, and the specks of lighter color.

Referring to the wild turkey (*M. g. silvestris*) Bendire says (*loc. cit.*, p. 116): "In shape, the eggs of the Wild Turkey are usually ovate, occasionally they are elongate ovate. The ground color varies from pale creamy white to creamy buff. They are more or less heavily marked with well-defined spots and dots of pale chocolate and reddish brown. In an occasional set these spots are pale lavender. Generally the markings are all small, ranging in size from a No. 6 shot to that of dust shot, but an exceptional set is sometimes heavily covered with both spots and blotches of the size of buckshot, and even larger. The majority of eggs of this species in the U. S. National Museum collection, and such as I have examined elsewhere, resemble in coloration the figured type of *M. gallopavo mexicanus*, but average, as a rule, somewhat smaller in size.

"The average measurement of thirty-eight eggs in the U. S. National Museum collection is 61.5 by 46.5 millimetres. The largest egg measures 68.5 by 46, the smallest 59 by 45 millimetres."

At the close of his account of *M. g. mexicanus* Bendire states that "The only eggs of this species in the U. S. National Museum collection, about whose identity there can be no possible doubt, were collected on Upper Lynx Creek, Arizona, in the spring of 1870, by Dr. E. Palmer, whose name is well known as one of the pioneer naturalists of that Territory.

"The eggs are ovate in shape, their ground color is creamy white, and they are profusely dotted with fine spots of reddish brown, pretty evenly distributed over the entire egg. The average measurements of these eggs is 69 by 49 millimetres. The largest measures 70.5 by 49, the smallest 67 by 48 millimetres.

"The type specimen (No. 15573, U. S. National Museum collection, Pl. 3, Fig. 15) is one of the set referred to above" (*loc. cit.* p. 119).

This set of three eggs I have personally studied; they are of *M. g. merriami*, and I find them to agree exactly with Captain Bendire's description just quoted.[42]

In the Ralph Collection (U. S. Nat. Mus. No. 27232; orig. No. 10/6) I examined six (6) eggs of *M. g. intermedia*. They are of a pale ground color, all being uniformly speckled over with minute dots of lightish brown. These eggs are rather large for turkey eggs. They were collected at Brownsville, Texas, May 26, 1894.

Another set of *M. g. intermedia* collected by F. B. Armstrong (No. 25765, coll. U. S. Nat. Mus.) are practically *unspotted*, and such spots as are to be found are very faint, both the minute and the somewhat large ones.

In Dr. Ralph's collection (U. S. Nat. Mus. No. 27080) eggs of *M. g. intermedia* are *short*, with the large and fine dots of a pale *orange yellow*. I examined a number of eggs and sets of eggs of *M. g. osceola*, or Florida turkey. In No. 25787 the eggs are short and broad, the ground color being pale whitish, slightly tinged with brown. Some of the spots on these eggs are unusually large, in a few places, three or four running together, or are more or less confluent; others are isolated and of medium size; many are minute, all being of an earth brown, varying in shades. In the case of No. 25787 of this set, the dark-brown spots are more or less of a size and fewer in number; while one of them (No. 25787) is exactly like the egg of Plate VI, Fig. 22; finally, there is a pale one (No. 25787) with *fine* spots, few in number in middle third, very numerous at the ends. There are *scattered large spots* of a dark brown, the surface of each of which latter are raised with a kind of incrustation. Another egg (No. 27869) in the same tray (*M. g. osceola*) is *small*, pointed; pale ground color with very fine spots of light brown (coll. W. L. Ralph). Still another in this set (No. 27868) is markedly *roundish*, with minute brown speckling uniformly distributed. There are nine (9) eggs in this clutch (No. 27868), and apart from the differences in form, they all closely resemble each other; and this is by no means always the case, as the same hen may lay any of the various styles enumerated above, either as belonging to the same clutch, or at different seasons.

As it is not the plan of the author of the present work to touch, in this chapter, upon the general habits of wild turkeys—their courtship, their incubation, the young at various stages, nesting sites, and a great deal more having to do with the natural history of the family and the forms contained in it—it would seem that what has been set forth above in regard to the eggs of the several subspecies in our avifauna pretty thoroughly covers this part of the subject.

Shortly after the last paragraph was completed I received a valuable photograph of the nest and eggs of *M. g. merriami*, and this I desire to publish here with a few notes, although in so doing it constitutes a departure from what I have just stated above in regard to the nests of turkeys.

This photograph was kindly furnished me by my friend Mr. F. Stephens of the Society of Natural History of San Diego, California, with permission to use it in the present connection. It has not to my knowledge been published before, though the existence of the negative from which it was printed has been made known to ornithologists by Major Bendire, who says, in his account of the "Mexican Turkey" in his *Life Histories of North American Birds* (*loc. cit.* p. 118): "That well-known ornithologist and collector,

Mr. F. Stephens, took a probably incomplete set of nine fresh eggs of this species, on June 15th, 1884. He writes me: 'I was encamped about five miles south of Craterville, on the east side of the Santa Rita Mountains in Arizona; the nest was shown to my assistant by a charcoal burner. On his approach to it the bird ran off or flew before he got within good range. He did not disturb it but came to camp, and in the afternoon we both went, and I took my little camera along and photographed it. The bird did not show up again. The locality was on the east slope of the Santa Rita Mountains, in the oak timber, just where the first scattering pines commenced, at an altitude of perhaps 5000 feet.'

"A good photograph, kindly sent me by Mr. Stephens, shows the nest and eggs plainly. It was placed close to the trunk of an oak tree on a hillside, near which a good-size yucca grew, covering, apparently, a part of the nest; the hollow in which the eggs were placed was about 12 inches across and 3 inches deep. Judging from the photograph the nest was fairly well lined."

In order to complete my share of the work, I will now add here a few paragraphs and illustrations upon the skeletal differences to be found upon comparison of that part of the anatomy of wild and domesticated turkeys. This is a subject I wrote upon many years ago; what I then said I have just read over, and I find I can do no better than quote the part contained in the "Analytical Summary" of the work. It is more or less technical and therefore must be brief, though it is none the less necessary to complete the subject of the present treatise.[43]

1. As a rule, in adult specimens of *M. g. merriami*, the posterior margins of the nasal bones indistinguishably fuse with the frontals; whereas, as a rule, in domesticated turkeys these sutural traces persist with great distinctness throughout life.

2. As a rule, in wild turkeys we find the craniofrontal region more concaved and wider across than it is in the tame varieties.

3. The parietal prominences are apt to be more evident in *M. g. merriami* than they are in the vast majority of domesticated turkeys; and the median longitudinal line measured from these to the nearest point of the occipital ridge is longer in the tame varieties than it is in the wild birds. Generally speaking, this latter character is very striking and rarely departed

from.

4. The figure formed by the line which bounds the occipital area is, as a rule, roughly semicircular in a domesticated turkey, whereas in *M. g. merriami* it is nearly always of a cordate outline, with the apex upward. In the case of the tame turkeys I have found it to average one exception to this in every twelve birds; in the exception, the bounding line of the area made a cordate figure as in wild turkeys.

5. Among the domesticated turkeys, the interorbital septum almost invariably is pierced by a large irregular vacuity; as a rule this osseous plate is entire in wild ones.

6. The descending process of a lacrymal bone is more apt to be longer in a wild turkey than in a tame one; and for the average the greater length is always in favor of the former species.

7. In *M. g. merriami* the arch of the superior margin of the orbit is more decided than it is in the tame turkey, where the arc formed by this line is shallowed, and not so elevated.

8. We find, as a rule, that the pterygoid bones are rather longer and more slender in wild turkeys than they are among the tame ones.

9. At the occipital region of the skull, the osseous structures are denser and thicker in the tame varieties of turkeys; and, as a whole, the skull is smoother, with its salient apophyses less pronounced in them than in the wild types. There is a certain delicacy and lightness, very difficult to describe, that stamps the skull of a wild turkey, and at once distinguishes it from any typical skull of a tame one.

10. I have predicted that the average size of the brain cavity will be found to be smaller and of less capacity in a tame turkey than it is in the wild one. In the case of this class of domesticated birds, as pointed out above, this would seem to be no more than natural, for the domestication of the turkey has not been of such a nature as to develop its brain mass through the influences of a species of education; its long contact with man has taught it nothing—quite the contrary, for the bird has been almost entirely relieved from the responsibilities of using its wits to obtain its food, or to guard against danger to itself. These factors are still in operation in the case of the

51

wild types, and the advance of civilization has tended to sharpen them.

From this point of view, then, I would say that mentally the average wild turkey is stronger than the average domesticated one, and I believe it will be found that in all these long years the above influences have affected the size of the brain-mass of the latter species in the way above indicated, and perhaps it may be possible some day to appreciate this difference. Perhaps, too, there may have been also a slight tendency on the part of the brain of the wild turkey to increase in size, owing to the demands made upon its functions due to the influence of man's nearer approach, and the necessity of greater mental activity in consequence.

Recently I examined a mounted skeleton of a female wild turkey in the collection of the United States National Museum, and apart from the skull it presented the following characters: There were fifteen vertebræ, the last one having a pair of free ribs, before we arrived at the fused vertebræ of the dorsum. Of these latter there were three coössified into one piece.

The sixteenth vertebra supports a pair of free ribs that fail to meet the sternum, there being no costal ribs for them. They bear uncinate processes.

Next we find four pairs of ribs that articulate with hæmapophyses, and through them with the sternum. There are two free vertebræ between the consolidated dorsal ones and the pelvis; and the pelvis bears a pair of free ribs, the costal ribs of which articulate by their anterior ends with the posterior border of the pair of costal ribs in front of them.

A kind of long abutment exists at the middle point on each, there to accommodate the articulation. There are six free tail vertebræ plus a long pointed pygostyle. The os furcula is rather slender, being of a typical V-shaped pattern, with a small and straight hypocleidium. With a form much as we find it in the fowl, the pelvis is characterized by *not* having the ilia meet the sacral crista in front. The prepubis is short and stumpy. The external pair of xiphoidal processes of the sternum are peculiar in that their posterior ends are strongly bifurcated.

Plate VII
Fig. 24. Nest of a wild turkey *in situ*. (*M. g. merriami.*) Photo by

Mr. F. Stephens, San Diego, California.

In the skeleton of the manus, the pollex metacarpal projects forward and upward as a rather conspicuous process. Its phalanx does not bear a claw, and on the index metacarpal the indicial process is present and overlaps the shaft of the next metacarpal behind it. In the leg the fibula is free, and extends halfway down the tibiotarsal shaft.

The hypotarsus of the tarso-metatarsus is grooved mesially for the passage of tendons behind, and is also once perforated near its middle for the same purpose. As I have already stated, the remainder of the skeleton of this bird is characteristically gallinaceous and need not detain us longer here. I would add, however, that the "tarsal cartilages" in the turkey extensively ossify.

CHAPTER V
BREAST SPONGE—SHREWDNESS

Nature has provided the old gobbler with a very useful appendage. Audubon calls it the "breast sponge," and it covers the entire upper part of the breast and crop-cavity. This curious arrangement consists of a thick mass of cellular tissue, and its purpose is to act as a reservoir to hold surplus oil or fat. It is quite interesting to study its function, and it is a very important one for the gobbler. This appendage is not found on the hen or yearling gobbler. At the beginning of the gobbling season, about March 1st, this breast sponge is full of rich, sweet fat, and the gobbler is plump in flesh; but as the season advances and he continues to gobble, strut, and worry the hens, his plumpness is reduced, and finally the bird becomes emaciated and lean. Often during the whole day he gobbles and struts about, making love to the hens, and at this time he eats almost nothing, being kept alive largely by drawing on his reservoir of fat. As the gobbler begins to grow lean, his flesh becomes rank and wholly unfit for food, and one should never be killed at this time. It is a fact that the young male turkeys gobble but seldom, if at all, the first year. Neither do these young birds possess the breast sponge, or reservoir to hold fat, and consequently they are unfit to mate with the hens. The hens visit the males every day or alternate days; consequently, if among the gobblers there are no mature birds, the eggs laid are not fertile. I wish every hunter, sportsman, and farmer could read these lines, and recognize the importance of sparing at least one of the adult male turkeys in each locality. The benefit of such a policy would soon be apparent in the increase of the turkeys. I dwell at length on this point in order to make clear the necessity of sparing some old gobblers in each section.

It has frequently been stated that the wild turkey will not live and propagate within the haunts of man. This depends upon how the birds are treated. No bird or animal can survive eternal persecution. There is no trouble about the birds thriving in a settled community, if the proper territory is set apart for their use, and proper protection given. The territory should consist of a few acres of woodland, or of some broken ground, thicket, or swamp to afford a little cover. In such a retreat, a trio of wild turkeys may be turned loose, and in a few years, if properly protected, the vicinity would be stocked with them.

I have ample evidence that wild turkeys will not shrink from civilization. It is the trapping, snaring, baiting, and killing of all old gobblers that decimates their numbers, not the legitimate hunting by sportsmen.

Note the full chest of the gobbler on the left. This is the breast sponge. (Photographed in March)

The shrewdness of the turkey is shown by his having no fear of the peaceable farmer at the plow, no more than the crow or the blackbird has. The wild turkey will go into the open field and glean food from the stubble or upturned furrows in full view of the plowman. This I have often seen, and I will cite one incident of this kind, which came under my observation some time ago when hunting in the State of Mississippi. It was a clear, beautiful morning in the month of March. Three old turkeys were gobbling in different directions, along a creek in a swamp, which was about half a mile wide, with fields on each side. Having selected the one I thought the oldest and biggest, I approached it as near as I dared; then, hiding myself in the brush, I began to call. In a short time the other two birds quit gobbling and came quickly to the call, while the one I had chosen continued his gobbling, but in the same place as when first heard. Suddenly I heard "*Put-put*" directly behind me; turning my head, I saw, within twenty paces of me, a fine gobbler. "*Put*"—then he was gone. This caused the one gobbling in front of me to become suspicious. He refused to come an inch nearer, and, having heard that alarm, "*put*," he began to make a detour in order to gain a certain heavily wooded ridge. To do this, without getting too near the spot where he heard the warning cry of his comrade, he had to go over a high rail fence, going through a part of the field just plowed up, while the plowman was there at work in his shirt sleeves, not over one hundred yards away and in full view of the gobbler. The man was moving all the time and frequently holloaing to his mules, "Whoa," "Gee," or "Haw," in such a loud voice that one could hear him a long distance. The turkey would gobble every time the plowman would holloa. He appeared to be perfectly fearless of the plowman, but was employing all his sagacity to avoid the spot where I was. I could not understand this at first, but discovered the reason a little later. The bird had reached the field and was flanking me, but I could not see it on account of the undergrowth. I rose, and by making a detour of about two hundred yards around the angle of the field, keeping well in the woods, I finally discovered the gobbler striding sedately across the field between me and the plowman, who was busily engaged in attending to his furrows, still loudly holloaing from time to time. The gobbler at intervals stopped, strutted, gobbled, and then proceeded on its way. Seeing that I could get no nearer to him, I waited until he was about to cross the fence, when I dropped by a stump, lifted my rifle, and waited for him to mount the fence. This he was some time in doing, but I finally heard the *flop, flop*, when his fine form with long, pendent beard was seen broadside on by me on the top rail, about eighty-five yards away. In a second the bead of my rifle covered the spot at the wing, and, as I fired, the bird tumbled dead into the field. It was a grand old specimen, and on examining it dry blood was discovered where a buckshot had passed through its leg. There was another shot across the rump, and a third had creased the back of the neck near the head. In my opinion, the bird hearing the "*put-put*" of the gobbler who came up behind me suspected a hidden enemy, and, having lately been wounded, thought it best to give suspicious places a wide berth.

There are thousands of acres in the South which were once cultivated, but which are now abandoned and growing up with timber, brush, and grass. Such country affords splendid opportunity for the rearing and perpetuation of the wild turkey. These lands are vastly superior for this purpose than are the solid primeval forests, inasmuch as they afford a great variety of summer food, such as green, tender herbage, berries of many kind, grasshoppers by the million, and other insects in which the turkeys delight. Such a country also affords good nesting retreats, with brier-patches and straw where the nest may be safely hidden, and where the young birds may secure safe hiding places from animals and birds of prey; but alas! at present not from trappers, baiters, and pot hunters. Check these, and the abandoned plantations of the South would soon be alive with turkeys.

CHAPTER VI
SOCIAL RELATIONS—NESTING—THE YOUNG BIRDS

The wild turkey differs in its domestic relations from the majority of birds, for it does not take one partner or companion, or pair off in the spring, as do most gallinaceous birds. Charles Hallock has stated that turkeys pair off in the spring. I beg to differ with Mr. Hallock. The male turkey does not confine himself to one mate.

He is a veritable Mormon or Turk, polygamous in the extreme, and desires above all a well-filled harem. He cares not a bit for the rearing or training of his family; in fact, it has been alleged that he follows his mates to their nests and destroys and eats the eggs. This I do not believe, nor will I accuse him of such conduct. He is a vain bird and craves admiration, and acts as if he were a royal prince and a genuine dude, and he will have admiration though it costs him his life. He is a gay Lothario and will covet and steal his neighbors' wives and daughters; and if his neighbors protest, will fight to the finish. He is artful, cunning, and sly, at the same time a stupendous fool. One day no art can persuade him to approach you, no matter how persuasively or persistently you call; the next day he will walk boldly up to the gun at the first call and be shot. He has no sentiment beyond a dudish and pompous admiration for himself, and he covets every hen he sees. He will stand for hours in a small sunny place, striving to attract the attention of the hens by strutting, gobbling, blowing, and whining, until he nearly starves to death. I believe he would almost rather be dead than to have a cloudy day, when he is deprived of seeing the sun shining on his glossy plumage; and if it rains, he is the most disconsolate creature on the face of the earth.

Nest located in thick brush on top of a ridge in Louisiana

The methods employed by the wild turkey hen in nesting and rearing a family do not differ materially from those of the tame turkey. The nest itself is a simple affair, fashioned as if made in a hurry, and consists of a depression scratched in the earth to fit her body comfortably, then a few dry leaves are scratched in to line the excavation. Again, the nest may be under an old fallen treetop or tussock of tall grass, or beside an old log, against which sundry brush, leaves, and grass have drifted, or in an open stubble field or prairie. There is one precaution the hen never neglects, however slovenly the nest is built; this is to completely cover her eggs with leaves or grass on leaving the nest. This is done to protect them from predaceous beasts and birds, particularly from that ubiquitous thief and villain, the crow.

The eggs, usually from eight to fifteen in number, are quite pointed at one end, a little smaller than the eggs of the domesticated turkey, showing considerable variation in size and shape. In color they are uniform cream, sometimes yellowish, and, when quite fresh, with a decided pink cast, spotted and blotched all over with reddish brown and sometimes lilac.

The period of incubation is four weeks. On its first appearance the young wild turkey is covered with a suit of light gray fluffy down, dotted with dusky spots, and with two dusky stripes from the top of the head, down the sides of the back to the rump; but this is soon replaced by a covering of deciduous feathers, and this in turn by the permanent suit at molting in August and September. The first crop of feathers which takes the place of the down grow very rapidly, assuming in their maturity the precise shape and color of the subsequent and permanent growth, and at three months the turkey is in appearance the same as one of nine months. The young bird of two or three pounds weight has the same outline of form as the yearling, but the little fellow in down bears a striking resemblance to a young ostrich. The deciduous feathers mature quickly, and the quill-ends dry before the young bird is a quarter grown; hence the feathers grow no more. But the bird grows until molting-time arrives, when the young fowl, if a gobbler, will weigh from seven to nine pounds. The molting season comes on apace, and the bird is out of humor; for its clothes, as it were, do not fit, the mosquitoes and ticks bite it, and the deciduous quills of the wings begin to get loose and drop out, one at a time at long intervals, so that some feathers are growing while others are falling. This is also true of the body covering. The tail becomes snaggled and awry, and at the time the young turkey presents anything but a pleasing appearance. The molting begins in August, and it is the last of December before the full second suit of feathers is completed. It is the irregular growth of the feathers that often deceives the hunter as to the age of the fowl. Once a friend of mine and I, after a morning's hunt, stopped to rest and got into our boat. He had three fine turkeys, the time being early in November, and he remarked that he wished he had killed at least one gobbler to put with his hens. On examination I showed him that two of his three were young gobblers and the third an old hen, although the birds were about the same size and the plumage almost identical.

The tuft or beard does not appear on the young gobbler even in the Southern climate until late in October or November, nor have I known them to gobble or strut at this early age, although the tame ones sometimes do. The gobbler's beard grows quite rapidly until the end of the third year, and then slowly until eleven or twelve inches long, when it seems to stop. It may be owing to its wearing off at the lower end by dragging on the ground while feeding; but a close inspection will not substantiate this, for the hairs at the extreme end of the beard are blunt and rounding, and do not indicate wear from friction. The young gobbler's beard is two inches long by the end of November of the first year of his life. By March it is three inches long and stands out of the feathers one inch. At the end of the second year it is five inches long, and at three years about eight inches long.

Hen, wild turkey, and three young. On account of the extreme shyness of the mother, young turkeys are very hard to photograph

Hens have beards only in rare cases, but not in one out of a hundred will a hen be found with one and then never more than four inches long. I have seen gobblers with two or three beards, and one at Eagle Lake, Texas, with five separate, long and distinct beards; but such cases are freaks. I once called up and killed a turkey hen on the banks of the Trinity River, in Texas, which was covered with precisely the same bronze feathers that distinguish the gobbler—the same thick, velvety black satin breast, and the same beautifully decorated neck and head, except the white turban cap of the gobbler. She had a five-inch beard and looked in every way like a gobbler,

59

except being smaller in size. She weighed twelve pounds and had the form of the hen, the legs of a hen, and was a hen, but the most gaudy and beautiful specimen I ever saw. Possibly this was a barren hen, as she had all the visible characteristics of the male, but she did not gobble, she yelped.

The parasite which troubles the turkey is much larger than those which infest chickens. It is yellow in color and crawls rapidly. Turkeys have a habit of rolling themselves in dust and ashes to remove vermin from the skin and feathers; but I believe a bath of dry wood ashes, where an old log or stump has been burned, is preferred by them on account of the cleansing effect of the ashes.

When the young turkeys are four or five months old they are fairly independent of their mother, and become quite self-reliant, so far as roosting, feeding, and flying into trees is concerned. They are not, however, entirely independent of their mother's care until fully grown, but usually the entire brood remains under her guidance more or less until December or January. At this time the young males begin to follow the ways of the old gobbler, separating from the females and going in bands by themselves; therefore there are at this time three classes of turkeys socially (if I may use the term) in the same district. These flocks will incidentally meet, and will feed and scratch together for an hour or so; they then separate into their respective classes and disappear in different directions with great system and little ado.

CHAPTER VII
ASSOCIATION OF SEXES

Once I saw fifteen gobblers feeding in a hollow between two ridges. I dismounted from my horse, crawling to the brow of the hill in order that I might peep over and have a good look at them. I had no gun with me at the time, so I lay upon the ground and watched the turkeys feeding and scratching for about two hours. They were apparently all of one flock; but finally a party of nine, all of which were old gobblers, having long beards that trailed upon the ground as they fed, withdrew in one direction, while the other six, which were young or yearling gobblers and beardless, departed in another direction. This was done without any signal that I could discern. A few days later, as I was passing the same place with my rifle, I found, right on the identical spot, the same fifteen gobblers, nine old ones and six young ones, scratching and feeding as before. They soon began to feed away from me, and as I saw they were to pass over a ridge, I fired at the nearest, which was about one hundred and twenty-five yards away, tumbling him over, and the rest of the flock ran away. Two weeks after this incident I was driving in the same woods for deer. The hounds flushed one detachment of this flock of turkeys (the nine old gobblers), which took refuge in the trees; and my brother, who was on a stand near where they lit, shot two of the turkeys as they perched in the tall pines within rifle shot of him. These birds were noble fellows, weighing twenty-one pounds each, and they were fat. This was in January.

As shown, the young gobbler will occasionally associate with the old ones, but he seldom remains long in their company. Why this is so I do not know, as I have never known them to quarrel, jostle, fight, or disagree in any way. I have come to the conclusion that the cause of the separation must be the want of congeniality between old age and youth. This division and separation into classes embraces about three months, December, January, and February, and part of March. The hens are more sociable and gregarious in their ways than the males, collecting in immense flocks. The flocks of the gobblers are seldom more than fifteen or twenty, while I have seen from

61

thirty to seventy-five hens in a single flock in which there was not a single male. I imagine the greater size of the flocks containing females to be on account of the gobblers being killed in far greater numbers than the hens. Just before the time of the final separation of the sexes, the young males, their sisters, their mothers, and other old hens that have lost their broods, associate in a very sociable manner, traveling and roosting together. Audubon says: "The turkey is irregularly migratory, as well as irregularly gregarious. In relation to the first of these circumstances, I have to state that whenever the mast in one part of the country happens to exceed that of another, the turkeys are insensibly led to that spot by gradually meeting in their haunts with more fruit the nearer they advance toward the places of greatest plenty. In this manner flock follows flock until one district is entirely deserted while another is overflowed by them, but as these migrations are irregular, and extend over vast expanse of country, it is necessary that I should describe the manner in which they take place. About the beginning of October, when scarcely any seed and fruit has yet fallen from the trees, the birds assemble in flocks and gradually move toward the rich bottom lands of the Ohio and the Mississippi. The males, or as they are commonly called, gobblers, associate in parties from ten to one hundred, and search for food apart from the females, while the latter are singly advancing, each with its brood about two thirds grown, or in connection with other families, often amounting to seventy or eighty individuals all intent on shunning the old cocks, which, even when the young brood have attained this size, will fight and often destroy them by repeated blows on the head." This last assertion of the great author I feel obliged to criticise. In my vast experience with the turkey I have never met with anything to justify such a statement. I have never seen an old gobbler attempt to fight a young one, from the egg to maturity. It is wholly unnatural from the fact that the old birds are never in a bellicose temper except during the love season or gobbling time in the spring, when jealousies arise from sexual instincts. Not in any instance, however, have I known of one turkey killing another. I have often seen two old gobblers strut up to each other, blow, puff, and rub their sides together. I watched, expecting to see a crash, but there was not a motion to strike, and this was in the love season while there was a bevy of hens all around. They do not fight in the summer, fall, and winter, but of course now and then old gobblers will fight in the beginning of the mating season.

The young broods and their mothers do not associate at any time with the old gobblers, except as I have described, neither do they run away from them in fear. If all that Audubon and other writers say about the wild gobbler were believed, he would be universally regarded as the most bellicose and brutal villain in the bird world; for, according to various writers, he spends the greater part of his time making war on his own kind, besides murdering his tender offspring. Certainly there is no bird more affectionate to its female under the same condition, or more gallant and proud of her company, and it does not seem likely that he would wilfully destroy in cold blood his own family.

The old hens that have not succeeded in raising a brood of their own will join hens who have, and assist in rearing the young. Again, Audubon says: "When they come upon a river they partake themselves to the highest eminence, and there often remain a day or two as if in consultation. During this time the males are heard gobbling, calling, and making much ado, and are seen strutting about as if to raise the courage to a pitch before the emergency of crossing."

The beginning of the strut. These gobblers are strutting before the camera hidden by brush in an endeavor to attract the hen turkey whose love call the camera man is imitating with his "caller."

I will say in this connection that turkeys may so act in rare instances, if the stream be exceptionally wide, thus delaying their progress for an hour; for turkeys do not like to fly under any conditions, nor will they use their wings save when necessary. But I have never seen a river that they could not easily cross, starting at the water's edge, rising as they fly, and alighting in the tops of the trees on the opposite bank. Mr. J. K. Renaud, of New Orleans, and I, while paddling a skiff up a small lake in Alabama, once counted a flock of sixteen turkeys flying across the lake some distance ahead of us. We noticed that they just barely skimmed over the water and rose to the top of a higher ridge on the opposite side, where they alighted, and not even one touched the water. This lake was probably three hundred yards wide.

Audubon says: "Even the females and young assume something of the pompous demeanor, spreading their tails and running around each other, purring loudly, and making extravagant leaps. I have seen this running round, purring, dancing, and 'ring-around a rosy' in the spring, but not to any extent at any other time."

As many of my readers have never had the opportunity or pleasure of reading the beautiful and expressive lines of Audubon on the wild turkey, I will be pardoned if I introduce some extracts from this great author. He says: "As early as the middle of February they [the turkeys] begin to experience the impulse of propagation. The females separate and fly from the males. The latter strenuously pursue and begin to gobble, or utter the notes of exultation. The sexes roost apart, but at no great distance from each other. When a female utters a call-note, all the gobblers within hearing return the sound, rolling note after note with as much rapidity as if they intended to emit the last and first together, not with the spread tails as when fluttering round the hens on the ground, or practising on the branches of trees on which they have roosted for the night, but much in the manner of the domestic turkey when an unusual noise elicits its singular hubbub."

By this he means, when the wild gobbler on the roost hears the call of the hen, he gobbles, and dances on the limb without strutting, the same as the tame gobbler will gobble when hearing a shrill whistle or other sudden acute sound, without evincing any amorous feelings; but it is not always so. I have often seen the wild gobbler strut on his roost, and I have shot them in such an act when in full round strut.

Audubon also says: "If the call of the hen is from the ground, all the males immediately fly toward the spot, and the moment they reach it, whether the hen be in sight or not, spread out and erect their tails, draw the head back on the shoulders, depress the wings with a quivering motion, and strut pompously about, emitting at the same time successions of puffs from their lungs, stopping now and then to listen and look, but whether they spy females or not, continue to puff and strut, moving with as much celerity as

64

their ideas of ceremony seem to admit."

Now, here are some of the greatest errors of the great naturalist in all his turkey lore, or else the wild turkey gobbler has materially changed his ways. The gobblers do not immediately fly to the call of the hen, and no turkey hunter of experience will admit this.

There are perhaps instances, extremely rare ones though, when a gobbler will fly instantly to a hen on hearing her call, or even at sight of her. Only in two instances in my life have I witnessed it, and on both occasions the gobblers were young birds two years old, and acted a good deal like a schoolboy with his first sweetheart—who smiles and laughs at everything she says and does. With the young turkey it may be his first gobble on hearing the quaver of the hen. He is made crazy, and may unceremoniously rush to any sound that in the least resembles the cry of the hen, without a thought of what he is about or of the possible consequences. This is generally the kind of gobbler the novice in calling bags as his first, a two-year-old with a five-inch beard.

In the early morning, during the spring, a gobbler will fly from his roost to the ground, strutting and gobbling, whether a hen is in sight or not; this is done to attract the hens, and it is then you will hear the puffs to which Audubon refers. This sound is produced by the gobbler in expelling the air from its lungs, at the beginning of the strut, the sounds and motions of which have never been satisfactorily described. While going through the strut the gobbler produces a number of notes and motions that are of interest; first, the wings are drooped until the first six or eight feathers at the end of the wings touch the ground; at the same time the tail is spread until like an open fan and erected at right angles to the body; the neck is drawn down and back until the head rests against the shoulder feathers, and the body feathers are all thrown forward until they stand about at right angles to their normal place. At the same time the body is inflated with air, which, with the drooping wings, spread tail, and ruffled feathers, gives the bird the appearance of a big ball. Having blown himself up to the full capacity of his skin, the gobbler suddenly releases the air, making a puff exactly as if a person, having inflated the cheeks to their full capacity, suddenly opens the mouth. As the puff is given, the bird steps quickly forward four or five paces, dragging the ends of the stiff wing feathers along the ground, making a rasping sound; he throws forward his chest, and, gradually contracting the muscles, forces the air from his body with a low, rumbling boom, the feathers resuming their normal position as the air is expelled. Three distinct sounds are produced: "*Puff, cluck, b-o-o-r-r-r-m-i.*" At the termination of the gobbling season the primaries of the wings, which are used to produce the cluck, are badly worn by the continued dragging on the ground.

"While thus occupied," continues Audubon, "the males often encounter each other, and desperate battles take place, ending in bloodshed and often in the loss of many lives, the weaker falling under repeated blows inflicted upon their heads by the stronger. I have often been much diverted while watching two males in fierce conflict by seeing them move alternately back and forth as either had obtained a better hold, their wings dropping, tails partly raised, body feathers ruffled, and heads covered with blood. If in their struggle and gasps for breath one of them should lose his hold, his chance is over, for the other, still holding fast, hits him violently with his spurs and wings and in a few moments brings him to the ground. The moment he is dead the conqueror treads him underfoot; but what is stranger, not with hatred, but with all the emotions he employed in caressing the female."

I differ with Audubon, not in the case of the conqueror using affectionate conduct upon a fallen foe, should he get him down, as that is truly a freak with them; but I have not seen such a performance with wild birds, although I have noticed the domestic gobbler act similarly toward the body of a dead wild gobbler that I had placed before him on the ground. I have very often brought such a bird into the presence of a tame one, when, at the very sight of the dead bird on my back, the tame one would begin to droop his wings, purr, bow his neck, and bristle for a fight, and at once pounce upon the dead bird, even pounding me until I laid it down and allowed him to vent his rage by pounding it. After this he would begin to strut and gobble, and the red of his head becoming intense he would go through the caressing motions. More often though, under the circumstances, the tame bird would, at the sight of the dead wild gobbler, retire a little way and strut in a furious manner for an hour or two. This does not apply to one instance or individual, but many times in many places. I must differ with Audubon as to the results of these conflicts ever being fatal. I have seen many encounters as he describes, but have never in all my life seen one gobbler killed by another, or even crippled, although I have seen two or three birds fight together for hours at a time. Nor have I ever found a gobbler dead in the woods as a result of such an encounter, or even in a worried condition. I have killed many old gobblers and found their heads and necks covered with blood, with spur punctures all over their breasts; but this never stopped them from gobbling, nor are these wounds deep, as the spur, which is an inch and a quarter long in the oldest of them, can only penetrate the skin of the body after passing through the heavy mail of thick, tough feathers.

Another proof that the gobblers in my hunting grounds were not killed this way is that I should have missed them. How would you know? you might ask. In the same way that a stock owner knows when he misses a yearling from his herd. Being constantly in the woods, I knew every gobbler and his age (at least the length of his beard) within a radius of several miles, although there be three in one locality and five in another. During the time they were in flocks or bands, if one were missing, surely I would find it out ere long; and it has never yet happened that, when one was missing, I could not trace it to a gunshot and not to turkey homicide. I will not flatly dispute that there have been such incidents as cited by Audubon, met with by others; but I do claim that murder is not common among turkeys, and such incidents must be extremely rare, or I would have witnessed them. I can see no way by which one turkey can kill another; for, as I have said before, the spur is not long enough except to barely penetrate the thick feathers, and the biting and pinching of the tough skin on the neck and head could not cause contusion sufficient to produce death, nor are the blows from the wings sufficiently severe to break bones.

CHAPTER VIII
ITS ENEMIES AND FOOD

No bird on earth can boast of more or a greater variety of enemies than the wild turkey. The chief of them all is the genus *Homo*, with his sundry and sure methods of destruction. After man comes a host of wild beasts and birds, including the lynx, coyote, wolf, fox, mink, coon, skunk, opossum, rat, both golden and white-headed eagles, goshawk, Cooper's and other hawks, horned owl, crow, etc., all of whom prey more or less upon the poor birds from the egg to maturity. There is never a moment in the poor turkey's life that eternal vigilance is not the price of its existence. Still, many pass the gauntlet and live to a great age, the limit of which no man has discovered. I have been a lifelong hunter of all sorts of game indigenous to the Southern States, and I have never seen or heard of a wild turkey dying a natural death, nor have I heard of any disease or epidemic among them; and were it not for the eternal war upon this fast-diminishing species, especially by man, they would be as plentiful now as fifty years ago.

The first in the list of natural enemies of the turkey, if we admit the testimony and belief of nearly every turkey hunter, is the common lynx or wildcat, often known as bobcat. Many hunters believe that of all the enemies of the wild turkey the wildcat is the chief. In all my experience I have never seen a turkey attacked by a cat, nor have I ever seen the skeleton of a turkey which had been killed and eaten by cats. I have never seen a cat crouching and creeping up on a turkey, nor have I had one of them come to me while calling, and I have had more than fifty years' experience in turkey hunting in all the Gulf States where the cat is common. Numerous persons of undoubted veracity, however, have assured me that they have seen cats creep up near them while calling turkeys, and in some instances the evidence seems conclusive that the cat had no other business than to steal up and pounce upon the turkey. Like any other carnivorous beast, the lynx may partake of turkey as an occasional repast, if they are thrown in his way, but this is an exception and not the rule.

My brother, who is a well-known turkey hunter in Mississippi, has furnished me with the following incident: As he sat on the bank of a small lagoon, in the early morning, with his back against a log that lay across the lagoon, calling a gobbler which was slow to come, he heard the soft tread of something on the log very near his head, on the side next to the lagoon. Turning slowly, he saw a large cat within three feet of him, apparently having crossed the water in an attempt to spring upon the supposed turkey that had been yelping on that side. When my brother faced the cat, it beat a rapid retreat, and my brother, springing to his feet, waited until the cat left the log, thus turning its side toward him, when he fired, killing it on the spot. There is little doubt but that in another minute the cat would have jumped on my brother's head. Another time he was sitting calling a gobbler, when suddenly he heard a growling and purring noise in the cane near him. Presently there appeared three large cats, but they seemed to be playing or having a love feast, as they walked about, sprang upon each other, squalled, scratched, springing up the trees, then down again, until he broke up the fun by a couple of shots that laid out a brace of them. Another time he was calling a gobbler which was gobbling vehemently, when suddenly there was a great commotion among the turkeys, clucking and flying up in trees. A cat then appeared out of the cane and was shot.

Now, does this prove, in either of the last two cases, that the cats were trying to catch the turkeys? By no means. For, had the cats been trying to get a turkey, they would not have shown themselves. I believe the cats were simply lounging about in quest of rabbits or squirrels, and happened to pass near the birds, which became frightened at the appearance of so uncanny a visitor. In the last incident, had the cat been attempting to seize or pounce upon the turkeys, they would not have gobbled again, but would have left the place in a hurry. Another reason why I claim that wildcats do not habitually feed on turkeys is, that one may find a given number of turkeys in a piece of woodland, and never miss one from the flock, unless trapped or killed by a gun—that is, after they are grown.

I will cite another incident connected with the habits of the lynx or wildcat that came under my observation while in quest of wild turkeys in the State of Alabama, in company with my friend John K. Renaud, of New Orleans, an enthusiastic and inveterate sportsman. We were in the

Tombigbee Swamp, and one morning, while sitting together in a fallen treetop, calling turkeys, our backs against a log, I felt something soft against my hip. As it felt a little warmer than the earth should feel, I pulled away the leaves with my hands, and there lay an immense cane rabbit dead. Upon pulling it out, I found its head was eaten off close to the shoulders, with no other part touched. This was the work of a lynx. Two days after, we were sitting by another log, not over a hundred yards from the first spot, and for the same purpose. I found there a similar object, a large rabbit freshly killed and half eaten, the head and forepart of the body gone. That was the work of a cat. There were plenty of turkeys frequenting that ridge every day, but never one of them was taken by a lynx, as I knew positively just how many gobblers and hens there were in that piece of woods.

I do not think wildcats ever eat the eggs of the turkey when they come across a nest of them; they may catch the sitting birds, but all other animals named in the foregoing list eagerly eat the eggs, if they are lucky enough to find the nests; this is also true of the crow, who, on locating a nest, will watch until the mother leaves it in search of food, when it will quickly destroy as many eggs as possible. All the animals and birds named will catch the young turkeys, and the larger birds and animals will kill grown turkeys when they can catch them.

Snakes give the turkey very little trouble. I do not believe any snake we have can swallow a turkey egg, except possibly the largest of the colubers (chicken snakes). I have never met one that was guilty of it, although I have seen them swallow the eggs of the tame turkey.

Mr. John Hamilton, who has had great experience as a turkey hunter, tells me of seeing horned owls catch turkeys in the Brazos Bottoms in Texas, a number of times, as follows:

On going into the woods before daylight, and, taking a stand near some known turkey roost, to be ready to call them on their leaving the roost, he has, a number of times, been led directly to the tree in which the turkeys were roosting by a horned owl who was after a turkey for breakfast. By walking quietly under the tree, and getting the birds outlined against the sky, he could see what was going on. Turkeys prefer to roost on limbs parallel to the ground, and the owl, selecting a hen perched on a suitable limb, would alight on the same limb between her and the trunk of the tree, moving sedately along the limb toward the victim, and when very near her would voice a low "*who, who.*" The turkey, not liking the nearness of such a neighbor, who spoke in such sepulchral tones, would reply, "*Quit, quit,*" and move farther out on the limb. After a few moments the owl would again sidle up to the hen, repeating his first question, "*Who, who.*" "*Quit, quit,*" would answer Miss Turkey, moving a little farther out on the limb. This would be kept up until the end of the limb was reached and the turkey would be obliged to fly, and then the owl would catch her. From personal observation I know horned owls always push chickens from the roosts and catch them while on the wing.

A great destroyer of the turkey is rain and long wet spells, just after they are hatched in the months of May and June. I have always noticed that, if these months were reasonably dry, there would be plenty of turkeys and quail the following fall. After all, the weather controls the crops of turkeys more than all else.

The local range of the wild turkey varies in proportion as the food supply is generous or scanty. If food is plentiful, the turkey remains near where hatched, and does not make extensive rambles, its daily journeys being limited to a mile or so, and often to not a fourth of that distance. I can not agree with writers who claim that wild turkeys are constantly on the move, travelling the country over with no intention of ever stopping. Of course, when the food supply is limited and scant, as during the seasons of dearth of mast, the turkeys are necessarily compelled to wander farther in order to secure sufficient food; but they will always return to their native haunts when their appetites are appeased.

The chief of all his enemies is the "Genus homo"

In the early morning, all things being favorable, their first move after leaving the roost is in search of food, which search they undertake with characteristic vigor and energy, scratching and turning over the dry leaves and decaying vegetation. Two kinds of food are thus gained: various seed or mast, fallen from the trees and bushes, and all manner of insects, of both of which they are very fond, and which constitute a large part of their food supply. There is no bird of the gallinaceous order that requires and destroys more insects than wild turkeys. They will scratch with great earnestness over a given space, then, all at once, start off, moving rapidly, sometimes raising their broad wings and flapping them against their sides, as if to stretch, while others leap and skip and waltz about. Then they will go in one direction for some distance. Suddenly, one finds a morsel of some kind to eat, and begins to scratch among the leaves, the whole flock doing likewise, and they will keep this up until a large space, perhaps half an acre of land, is so gone over. What induces them to scratch up one place so thoroughly and leave others untouched would seem a mystery to the inexperienced; but close observation will show that such scratching indicates the presence of some kind of food under the leaves. It may be the nuts of the beech, oak, chestnut, chinquapin, black or sweet gum tree, pecan nut, grape, or muscadine seed. If one will observe the scratchings, it will be seen that they occur under one or another of such trees or vines. Thus they travel on, stopping to scratch at intervals until their crops are filled.

Under certain conditions, wild turkeys are compelled to seek numerous sources to obtain a supply of food, as when there is a failure of the mast crop, which affords the principal supply of their food, or when there is an overflow of the great swamps or river bottoms, which turkeys so often inhabit. When such overflows occur, the turkeys are either forced to take up their abode in the trees, or to leave their feeding ground and retreat to the high lands that are not overflowed. In the latter case there is little trouble in procuring food by scratching in the dry leaves or gleaning in the grain fields. But turkeys are hard to drive from their haunts, even by high waters, and more often than not they will stubbornly remain in the immediate locality of their favorite swamps and river bottoms by taking to the trees until the waters have subsided; they will persistently remain in the trees even for two or three months, with the water five to twenty-five feet in depth beneath them. At such times they subsist upon the green buds of the trees upon which they perch, and the few grapes and berry seeds that may remain attached to the vines which they can reach from the limbs. It is truly remarkable how long these birds can subsist and keep in fair flesh under such conditions. There is a critical time during these overflows, when turkeys are hard pressed in that they may obtain sufficient food to sustain life; this is when the rivers overflow in December, January, or February, before the buds have appeared or have become large enough to be of any value as food. Under these conditions they must fly from tree to tree until they reach dry ground, or starve to death.

Although I have never known of a gobbler being thus starved to death, I have seen them so emaciated they could hardly stand. One incident of this sort I will relate: I found four very large old gobblers in an overflowed swamp on the Tombigbee River in Alabama, and as it was in February, it was too early in the year for herbage to begin the spring growth. The river had overflowed the bottoms suddenly, and it was a long way to dry land, perhaps three miles, so the turkeys could get little or nothing to sustain life. I shot one of these gobblers, not thinking of their probable condition, and found I had bagged a skeleton.

If the bottoms are not over three miles wide, turkeys will usually, on approach of rising water, start for the dry ridges farther back from the river, and there remain until the waters steal upon them, when they will fly into the trees. Sometimes a ridge is an island at sundown when they go to roost, but is covered during the night, and when the morning comes there is no dry land in sight for the poor birds to alight upon. This is bewildering to them and presents a new state of affairs. If there be an old mother hen in the flock, she will at once take in the situation, and by certain significant clucks and a peculiar cackle, which is a part of their elaborate language, she will take wing and fly two or three hundred yards in the direction of dry land, alighting in the trees, when, after a rest, with another cluck or two, the party will continue in the same direction. This is kept up until the dry land is reached, when, with wild acclaim and a general cackle of exultation, they all alight on the ground and proceed at once, at a fearful rate, to scratch up the leaves in search of food.

The hunter, aware of these habits after the swamps begin to overflow, will lose no opportunity for an early visit to the hummock at the margin of the backwaters. The turkeys do not remain near the edge of the overflow for any length of time, but very soon extend their range farther into the high forests and fields. They seem to know instinctively that it is unsafe to linger near the edge of the water.

In case the overflow occurs in March or April, when the trees are full of fresh buds and blossoms, the turkeys have an easy time, living in the treetops, fluttering from branch to branch, gathering the tender buds and young leaves of such trees as the ash, hackberry, pin oak, and the yellow bloom of the birch, all of which are favorite foods, while of the beech and some other trees it is the fringe-like bloom they eat. They will remain in the trees out of sight of land for months if they have plenty of buds and young leaves to eat, and keep in fair flesh; but the flesh is not so palatable as when feeding on mast or grain.

I once knew a flock of fifteen turkeys to remain in trees above an overflow for two months. I could see them daily from my cabin on the bank of a lake in Alabama, and could sit at my table and watch them fluttering as they fed on the hackberry buds. They were in sight of a dry, piney wood, and a flight of three hundred yards across a lake would have taken them to the dry land, but not once did they seem inclined to go to it. They remained in the trees until the water went down, and the next I saw of them was in an open plantation, with the lake on one side and the river on the other. The water had barely left the surface in places, and it was muddy and sloppy. They never once went to dry land, but returned to their swamp haunts as the water abated.

On one occasion, as I was going down the river in my skiff, I saw and passed a great number of wild turkeys, one hundred or more, in small flocks in the timber near and along the river banks. The adjoining swamps were overflowed, with no land above the water. Most of these turkeys were sitting in cottonwood trees immediately on the river banks or a little way out in the timber, eating the buds. Many of them were in the trees that hung over the river, and, although most of the trees were leafless, thus exposing the turkeys to view, they remained there quite unconcerned while steamboats passed right by them. As I had three turkeys already in my boat, I felt no desire to molest them as I drifted by and under them. I passed right under some fine gobblers on their perches, not over thirty feet up, and they only looked curiously down at me; they seemed to be busily engaged in feeding, and sailed from tree to tree, keeping up a great stir and racket. It is a beautiful sight to watch a flock of wild turkeys budding, especially on beech buds. The branches of the beech trees are long and so limber that the birds with all their efforts can barely hold on to the tiny twigs while they gather their food; hence they are kept in a constant wobble and flutter, bobbing up and down with their wings spread out to sustain an equilibrium, and their broad tails waving and tossing, bringing them into all manner of attitudes, thus enabling the hunter to see and hear them a quarter of a mile through the timber. Some get upon very small limbs, then stretch out their long necks and pick the buds; others will spread out both wings for support and lie prone on a bunch of twigs while they feed. There is little or no trouble for the hunter to approach a flock so engaged and pick off his choice. They are so bent on eating that they take no note of what is going on around them; even if over dry land they will often remain in the trees half a day eating buds, if other food is scarce, and when tired or satiated they will sit calmly on some large limb and go to sleep or preen their feathers. This is one of the best opportunities afforded the crafty hunter with his good rifle to steal up behind a tree and deliberately drop one, as at this time the leaves are too small to afford much cover, and the turkeys are exposed to open view, giving the prettiest shots imaginable for the rifle. While this is one of the most successful and easiest ways of securing turkeys, there are few hunters who know enough about it to take advantage of it. Persons will often pass under trees in a turkey locality, when suddenly one or more turkeys will fly out. The hunter looks up, but sees only the turkeys on the wing, and cannot understand why they were in the trees at that time of day, as he has not flushed any. He wonders how they came to be there and does not know they were up there budding, having probably been there all the morning.

The budding season lasts but a short time, if the birds are not forced to it by an overflow. On dry land it lasts a month or six weeks, for by that time the buds have matured into full-grown leaves, and are too old and tough for the birds to eat.

CHAPTER IX
HABITS OF ASSOCIATION AND ROOSTING

After obtaining a supply of food, the wild turkeys become moody and careless, lounging about the sunny slopes if the weather be cool, or if it be hot, seeking the shade of the hummock or thicket, preening their feathers or wallowing in the dust. They thus pass the middle hours of the day in social harmony and restful abandon. About three or four o'clock in the afternoon the line of march is resumed in the direction of the roosting place, and they gather their evening meal as they journey along. They are excellent timekeepers, usually winding up the day at one of their favourite roosts; but in case this calculation is faulty and sundown overtakes them a mile or so from the desired spot, they will start on a run in single file, the old hens leading, and keep going rapidly until their destination is reached. They will then stop suddenly in a close group, peer about, uttering low purring sounds, while having a breathing spell from the long run. Having regained their composure, the old hens will sound several clucks in rapid succession, terminating in a guttural cackle, when the whole of the flock will take wing. With a wild roar, up they go in different directions, alighting in the largest trees with seldom more than two or three turkeys in a single tree. If they are not satisfied with their first selection of a roosting place, they will fly from tree to tree until a satisfactory place is found; then they settle down quietly for the night.

Wild turkeys have a preference for roosting over water, and they will often go a long way in order to secure such a roost. The backwater from the overflowing streams, when it spreads out widely through the standing timber of the river bottoms, affords them great comfort; also the cypress ponds to be found in our Southern river districts. They evidently fancy that there is greater safety in such places.

The turkey is happy when it can traverse the ridges, glades, and flats in a day's ramble from one watercourse to another, having a roosting place at one ridge one night and the next night at another. This sort of arrangement suits them admirably, as they dislike to roost in the same trees two or more consecutive nights. I have known them to make such regular changes as to roost in three or four different places in a week, bringing up at the same place not exceeding once or twice a week, and that on or about certain days. These are facts peculiar to the wild turkey, especially if localities are favorably arranged. But often they will roost very many nights near the same place. If the range is unlimited, however, they will seldom roost oftener than twice a week at a given spot. There are exceptions though, for I have known positively of old gobblers who took up their abode at a certain spot and roosted, if not in the same tree, in the same clump of trees, night after night and year after year with the persistent regularity of the peacock, which will roost on the same limb of a tree for ten or twenty years if undisturbed. When an old gobbler does take to this hermitlike custom, he is the most difficult bird to bag in the world. His life seems immune from attacks of any nature, and he seems to know the tactics of every hunter in the vicinity of his range. He keeps aloof from any old logs or stumps where an enemy may lurk, and never gobbles until daylight, so that he can take in every inch of his surroundings. I have killed from four to six old gobblers, in a given range, while trying to bag a certain stubborn old chap whose vigilance and good luck have saved him from bullets for years; but through patience and dogged persistence in the hunter he succumbed at last. Although some hold out longer in their reserved and retired course, I can truthfully say that I have yet to encounter one that can not be brought to the gun by fair and square calling. Many experienced and worthy hunters will criticise this assertion, and are honest in their convictions that I am in error; but I will take the dissenter to the haunts of the most astute old gobbler he may select, and call the turkey right up to the muzzle of his gun, or near enough to see the glint of his eye.

A flock may be met one morning on the skirts of the backwater from an overflow river bottom, probably a flock of hens and gobblers together. There would be a great commotion among them and a general mixing up, yelping, and gobbling. On visiting this place the next morning one would not be seen or heard. Crossing to another lake or backwater, one might find the whole flock, or possibly the gobblers, with not a hen around. If in the gobbling season, and the males are gobbling, in less than half an hour the hens would be among them, but if not in the gobbling season the former may not meet the latter again for a month, as in the spring the sexes have no more attraction for each other than were they birds of entirely different groups. Except in the spring you may flush and scatter a flock of hens and gobblers, and after a reasonable wait begin to call with the notes of the hen. Not a gobbler will answer or notice you at all, but the hens will reply by yelping, squealing, and clucking. The gobblers meantime are as stolid as an Indian and as silent as a dead stump. Wait until the hens have gone, then begin the lingo of the gobbler and you find another result.

An ideal turkey country. They will go a long way to roost in trees growing in water

Usually there are plenty of wild turkeys in the Southern river bottoms, in fall and winter, and there they remain until driven to the uplands by overflows, where they must subsist on pine mast, or remain in the trees over the water, and live on the young buds and tender leaves. I have repeatedly noticed this in the Tombigbee swamps in the State of Alabama. Those that do not go to the hills and pine forests will hug the margin of the overflow until the waters subside, when they will immediately return to their former haunts, however wet and muddy. When incubating time comes they seek the higher, dryer, and more open places, grassy and brush-covered abandoned plantations, there to carry out the duties of reproduction.

After the season of incubation is at an end the gobblers cease, almost entirely, associating with the hens, collecting, as the summer advances, in bands of from two to a dozen. Thus they remain all through the summer, autumn and winter, acting the rôle of old bachelors or widowers, and never separating unless disturbed by an enemy. The females care for and rear the young broods, returning to the swamps or hummocks in the fall, where their favorite food has matured and shed.

One of the last seasons I spent in the vicinity of the Tombigbee country in Alabama there were no grapes or muscadines in the bottoms, but a good pin oak crop of acorns, such as the turkeys like. In the higher woods there was a heavy black gum and berry crop, and there the turkeys were, while in the oak bottoms there was scarcely a flock.

During the summer months, old gobblers, like old bucks, having banded together, become very friendly and attached to each other, feeding in perfect harmony. They stroll together wherever their inclinations may lead them, and are then very shy and retiring. One seldom sees them in the summer, but when they do it is generally in an open prairie or old field, eating blackberries, wallowing in an old ash hole, or chasing grasshoppers. These old bachelors do not get fat until fall, although they have an ample supply of food. They are lean and ugly and forlorn looking until after the molting season is over, in August and September, and their new bronze suits are donned; they then begin to fatten, and by December are in excellent condition of flesh and feathers, continuing to improve until the gobbling season returns next spring. These confirmed old bachelors will not associate with the other turkeys, but the old hens that have had their nests broken up and have reared no broods will associate all winter with the young broods and their mothers. I have often observed that these old patriarchs, as a rule, never associate with any other age or sex of turkeys. In summer you will often see an old gobbler or two with a flock of hens early in the morning; but see the same flock three hours later and he is not with them. In the early morning hours of spring, while there is a general gobbling and strutting parade, all ages and sexes mingle in the exuberance of the season and hour; but when this outburst of frolic and revelry is over, the different bands return to the sterner business of the day, that of searching for food. The old gobblers remain gobbling, strutting, gyrating round, picking at and teasing each other, or strumming now and then with the tip of wings, until a riot is precipitated and a fight ensues, in which two become engaged, while the more peaceful or timid quickly leave the vicinity. The gladiators then begin a tug of war, and after a few blows and jams with wings and spurs, one seizes another by the loose skin of the head, which is very limp, affording an excellent hold; then No. 2 gets his opponent by the nape of the neck, and they pull, push, and shove, standing on tiptoes, prancing and hauling away, each endeavoring to stretch his neck as high as possible, as if determined to pull the other's head off, while both necks are twisted around each other, their wattles aglow with the red sign of anger, while their hazel eyes sparkle with wrath. They writhe, twist, and haul away, until perhaps a quarter of an acre of earth is trampled, and keep it up until the foolish combat ends from sheer exhaustion, when one of them runs away. The victor, if not too much used up, having recovered breath and strength, will set up a gobbling and strutting that will cause the leaves of the trees to tremble. He thus proclaims his victory and assumes the rôle of monarch of all he surveys.

A hermit. It would take an expert turkey hunter to circumvent this bird

By these fights one gobbler establishes his claim as lord of a certain range, which no other gobbler will dispute during the rest of the season.

Sometimes, though rarely, I have known an old monarch to take a companion gobbler into the very bosom of his harem, however strange this may appear. I have known of half a dozen instances of this nature where two old gobblers have formed an inseparable alliance and remained together staunch friends for years. Hens are seldom seen in their company and they are extremely difficult to call. I hunted one such brace three years, killing many other gobblers in the long effort to bag these two; never did I call them within gunshot, until one day by some accident they got separated, when it was no trouble to call and kill one of them; the other is, for all I know, alive now.

Such fights as I have described break up the social ring of old bachelors, and until the love season is over each male takes up a range to himself, calling to his side as many of the females within hearing of his voice as will come to him. Several gobblers can be heard in the morning gobbling within a radius of a few hundred yards, but each keeps to himself, and by frequent and persistent gobbling and strutting secures the society of such hens as may favor him with their presence.

After the disbanding of the old gobblers is the best time in the whole season to bring them to call, as they will come to almost any call, yelp, or cluck; except the mogul himself. His bigotry and vanity render him most indifferent to the seductive coquetry of the females, much less to human imitators. Being assured of, and satisfied with, a well-filled harem, he gives little care to the discordant piping of the hunter, or even the gentle quaver of a hen.

In this latitude—from 30 degrees to 33 degrees north—the gobbling season begins about the first week of March, ending the last of May, embracing about three months, though the time depends much on the thermal conditions of the spring. If the weather be dry and pleasant the season will not last as long as if wet and chilly.

CHAPTER X
GUNS I HAVE USED ON TURKEYS

The rifle is, *par excellence*, the arm for hunting the wild turkey under nearly all conditions. It matters little what calibre rifle is used. Years ago when I began to hunt turkeys the muzzle-loading round ball rifle was the only arm thought fit, and it surely did the work well and satisfactorily.

It is said that Davy Crockett when a boy was compelled by his father to shoot enough game in the morning to supply his dinner, and was allowed one load of powder and a ball to do it with. If he missed and got no game he got no dinner.

In the old days the .38 calibre, shooting a round ball, was about the proper size, with not too much twist in the rifle; one twist or turn in five feet was about the thing. Those rifles were reliable and did not lacerate the flesh unless too much powder was used.

Next came the breech-loading rifle with small charge of powder and heavy bullet; like the Winchester model '66 and Frank Wesson's single shot. These guns shot with remarkable correctness at short range, especially the Frank Wesson rifle; but none of them had enough velocity to do as fine shooting as is required in turkey shooting above 75 to 100 yards. With me the .38 calibre Wesson rifle did more certain work on old gobblers than any other rifle I have ever seen or used, nor was the powder charge sufficient to tear the flesh severely, but it would drive the bullet through two old gobblers.

The next best gun, and the best all-round shooting gun I ever used on turkeys was a .32-20 Winchester, model '73, but this gun tore the flesh badly.

The points to be desired in a turkey rifle are these: A bullet that will kill under ordinary conditions and at the same time leave a minimum trace through the bird; and a flat trajectory for fine shooting at 125 or 150 yards, as that is as far as one will be apt to risk a shot at them.

I found that the .32 calibre killed as well as the .50 calibre—I mean the .32-20—if the shot was placed right. It must be remembered that the skin of birds is very thin and delicate; the flesh under it, especially the breast, is extremely tender and juicy, and a rifle bullet passing through it with great velocity will spatter the flesh like soft butter, the bullet having mushroomed against the thick, hard feathers, or even on striking the flesh itself.

I believe the best rifle that could be made for turkey shooting would be .30 or .32 calibre, with about 15 grains of powder, and the weight of the bullet reduced as much as possible without injury to accuracy. It would have ample force and not tear the flesh and give even greater penetration than the .32-20. A turkey rifle should not mushroom its bullets, for, although the turkey possesses remarkable vitality, he is easily killed if shot in the right place.

As to shotguns, there is little choice so far as the shooting is concerned. Any good modern choke bored gun will answer—the choked being greatly to be preferred, as it concentrates its shot—which is a desirable quality in scoring—on the head or neck, the only mark for a shotgun on a turkey. No. 6 is by all means the size shot for this purpose; one barrel with No. 6 for the head, the other No. 3 or 4 for the body, is the proper thing.

Wing shooting turkey is so out of line with my idea of turkey hunting under any conditions that I have little to offer in that respect. To see a big, fine gobbler with his rich bronze plumage all messed up by shot and grime, legs and wings all broken and bloody, dangling about, is a disgusting sight to the true turkey hunter. The turkey is not built or in any way adapted to being so shot, but there are men so nervous and excitable that they cannot still-hunt turkeys. Such men must be going all the time, and their only chance is to scare up the birds and shoot them on the wing. They are not of the stuff that make good turkey hunters, and they will never succeed, no matter how they try. They have no patience to wait on the movement of a turkey when coming to the call, but can sit around a hotel all day spinning yarns, talking politics, and perhaps playing cards all night. This type of man can never become a quiet, contemplative, thoughtful turkey hunter.

Unless killed or wing broken, a turkey may receive while on the wing a mortal hurt and yet be lost, for it has such vitality that it will prolong its flight to such a distance as to be lost. At short range turkeys on the wing are easily dropped with a shotgun, but then the whole body is usually filled with shot. Hallock says: "If the hunter be so fortunate as to get within reach of a turkey, let him take deliberate aim at the head if he has a rifle, but the possessor of a shotgun should cover the whole body." To me this seems absurd, for it is the reverse of this that I would suggest to successfully kill the bird. Should the man of average nerve and excitability take aim at the head of a turkey with a rifle he will miss it. I have done it myself under certain conditions, and under ordinary circumstances I would not suggest that any sportsman take such chances.

The turkey hunter who uses his rifle gets more real enjoyment out of the sport than with any other arm. He gets more chances to kill the bird, because of the greater killing range of the rifle, and consequently is surer of his game, particularly if he is a marksman with a cool head, steady hand, and good vision. If one desires to be a first-class, all-round turkey hunter, my advice is to employ the rifle, and when a turkey is found, aim for the body, and that part of it that covers the vitals. If you do not do this you are likely to see your game running away as fast as his legs can carry him, for, unless your bullet has passed through his body, striking a vital part, the bird is likely to escape. If circumstances are such that you cannot procure a rifle, or are wedded to a shotgun, I should advise the use of No. 6 shot, and would recommend aiming at the head of the bird, unless they are young birds and quite near enough to make sure your shot. Do not use buckshot if you can procure any other. Should you use No. 5 or 6 shot and aim at the head, you will be surprised to learn at what range you can kill a turkey. Some hunters who use a shotgun prefer No. 6 in one barrel and No. 4 in the other, using one for the head and the other for the body. The reason that I do not recommend the use of buckshot in turkey hunting is because the vital parts of the turkey are very small, and at forty yards the chances of reaching these parts with buckshot are slim. Those who have tried buckshot at this range note that they have knocked their birds over nearly every time, but are surprised to see them get up and run away. This never happens if the sportsman uses a good rifle and places his bullet in the right place.

CHAPTER XI
LEARNING TURKEY LANGUAGE—WHY DOES THE GOBBLER GOBBLE

To learn to imitate the cry of a turkey is no great feat, if you have something to call with and know the sounds you wish to imitate. One can become proficient in the use of the call with reasonable effort; but to expect to call intelligently, without a proper knowledge of the interpretation of the notes produced, is as absurd as to read a foreign language and not know the meaning of the words. Unless you know the meaning of the gobble, the yelp, and cluck, in all their variations, you cannot expect to use the turkey language intelligently. Without such knowledge you will fail to interest the bird you try to call, unless by accident or sheer good luck you brought the cautious thing within sight. It is not desirable, though, that we depend upon luck; one should prefer skill in calling, so that he can at all times depend with a degree of certainty on accomplishing his purpose of fooling the bird. I was once hunting with a friend, and as we sat together by White Rock Creek calling an old gobbler; two or three other hunters, at different points but within hearing, were also calling, keeping the turkey continually gobbling. My friend asked why I did not call oftener, fearing the others would decoy the turkey away from us. I told him that I had already put in my call and the gobbler understood it, and the other fellows were calling by simply making sounds with no apparent meaning or reason, and when the gobbler got ready he would come to us. I then took out my pipe and had a smoke. Meantime the calling by the other hunters was going on at a terrific rate, and the gobbler was apparently tickling their ambition with his constant rattle and strut. Ere long he came directly to us and we shot him.

I have known men who could in practice yelp almost as well as the turkey, but when attempting to call the wild bird would do little better than the veriest novice. If such persons' confidence and ability to call did not fail them, their judgment would, and the opportunity would be spoiled by some absurd act.

It is not so much what one should do in calling, but what one should not do, as it is better to leave things undone unless done right. This subject requires the most minute and careful knowledge of turkey lore, and will require much of your patience before you are proficient, and I trust you will find in these lines more for your contemplation than you might suspect.

The conditions under which you call are daily varied, while the methods to be employed each time are quite complex. In spring the males are gobbling, and the love-call of the hen is then the one to use. In the fall and winter, when the turkeys are in flocks and do not gobble, this not being the love season, you do not then make love-call, but such as suits the occasion and the temper of the game.

First, as to gobbling: We will analyze that feature, as it involves great interest to the hunter. As a matter of fact, more people hunt the turkey during the gobbling season than at any other time, and strange to say get fewer turkeys, simply from the fact that the call is not understood.

Why do they go in quest of turkeys at that season? For the reason that they are much more easily located, as the gobbling of the turkey indicates its whereabouts, removing the necessity of spending much time in search of them; hence, were it not for the gobbling many hunters would never attempt to hunt the birds, knowing too well it would be useless.

The first and most important thing that you should impress on your mind is, that the turkey-cocks gobble for a reason.

Why does the gobbler stand in one spot and make a great ado? Every turkey, whether born in Florida or Mexico, does the same, and at the same period of the year, because his gobbling and strutting is to let the hens know where he is, and if he keeps it up every hen in hearing will come to him. The gobble of the male turkey is his love-call. In the early spring, when nature begins to unfold its latent energies and develop its dormant resources for creating new life, the old gobbler feels its impulses, and is not slow in asserting his place as leader of the grand aggregation of noisy choristers that make the deep solitudes of the forests ring to the echo. From some tall pine or cypress he loudly proclaims the approach of dawn. "*Gil-obble-obble-obble, quit, quit cut,*" comes the love-call from his excited throat, so suddenly and unexpectedly that all the smaller species within a hundred yards are dazed with fright. I often thought that, if he possessed any faculty of humor, he must be greatly amused at the commotion he creates all by himself.

Big woods in Louisiana where the old gobblers roam at will. A delightful place in which to camp

He stands erect on his high perch, peering in all directions to determine the next thing to do, or to ascertain the result of that already done, and it often happens that this is the last and only gobble he will produce that morning, owing to its being accidental. But he will stand upon the limb of his roost quietly looking about, and after preening his plumage for a few moments, and seeing that no enemy lurks near, he stoops, spreading his great curved wings, and silently as a summer's breeze leaves the tree and sails to the earth fifty to seventy-five yards from his perch. He stands perfectly still some moments until satisfied all is well, then he carefully places the tip of one wing on the other across his back once or twice, and walks slowly away to feed. A few mornings later, if the air be crisp, clear, and not too cold, he will gobble lustily many times before he flies down, for the first warm days of spring begin to arouse his animal instincts and he longs for the society of his mates.

He is now in the prime of turkeyhood, in his finest feather and flesh. He is fat and plump, hence this is the stage at which the hunter, most of all, prefers to bag him; but he is no easy game to secure just now.

If he ever were afraid of his own voice, step, or shadow, it is at this time; but the forest is ringing with a din of bird song, and it is impossible to restrain his impulse to "*gil-obble-obble-obble*." Making one or two quick steps, he raises his head and says "*put-put*," then stands perfectly still, his great hazel eyes scanning every leaf or bird that moves.

Why does he gobble? It is the call of nature to break up his loneliness and secure the society of his mates. Turkeys do not mate in pairs, they are polygamous, loving many wives.

I wish to direct attention to the common and erroneous belief, even among expert turkey hunters, that it is the call-note of the hen that brings the sexes together. This is incorrect. It is the call of the male. It was after years of study that I discovered this fact, which, once plain to my mind, assured my success as a turkey hunter. I found that the gobbler was doing the same thing I was doing; I was struggling with all my ability and tact to draw him out, while he was playing the same game on me; it was a question of who had the greater patience. If I remained and insisted on his approach, he would yield and come to me. Here is his customary method: At the very break of day, the weather being favorable, he begins to gobble in the tree in which he is roosting. The gobbling is produced at very irregular intervals, sometimes with long, silent spaces between, at others in rapid succession. Some turkeys gobble a great deal more than others. Some will gobble but once or twice before they come down, and gobble no more that day; others will not gobble until they fly down, and then keep it up for hours. Some will gobble all day from sunrise to sunset. All these various idiosyncrasies the knowledge of the hunter must meet. Some will come to the yelp or cluck at the first imitation of the sound, while others will take hours to make up their minds whether to come at all. Take it all together, the gobbler has most obstinate ways, purposely or not; the wily hunter must bring all his faculties to bear if he would outwit him.

If the old turkey begins to gobble on the roost at the early dawn and to strut (although all do not strut in the trees), he will gobble, watch, and wait, hoping he may catch sight of the female—located by her responsive yelp or cluck—that may be roosting in a tree near him, or one approaching on foot or flying toward him through the timber. If not so fortunate, he will usually fly to the ground, scan the surroundings with his keen eye a moment or so, then drop his wings, spread his semicircular tail, strut, and gobble. Then he lets his dress slowly down as the spasmodic paroxysm subsides, listens, and looks, gobbles a time or two, listens again, and struts, and so on. If he sees no hen or hears no sound resembling that which he desires, he begins to calmly walk toward his feeding grounds, gobbling at long intervals; he then usually stops for the day. This applies to the first weeks of the gobbling season, and he is quite easily called then, as it is too early for the hen to crave his attentions; but later it all changes.

The hens seek his presence as the procreative impulses begin to stir them. The gobbler then will take up a chosen territory in a certain piece of woods, the most favorable to required conditions, and roost in the vicinity nearly every night, that is, in case he has secured a fair harem of six or eight hens; but if he is not so fortunate he will run all about the country, having no special place to spend the night. But now we are contemplating the gobbler who has been so fortunate as to secure a fair-sized harem, and has confined himself to one locality, in which he will peaceably and contentedly remain all the gobbling season. I have heard them gobble late in June when they have one or two hens with them, who evidently have had their nests and eggs destroyed and are again associating with the males. It is usual for the hen to visit the gobbler every morning, staying in his company only for a short time; and when she departs he follows her slowly a few steps, then begins to strut and gobble violently until she is out of sight. He knows his complement of hens, and does not cease to strut and gobble until all hens come to him; he then quits gobbling and strutting and steals away to feed on tender leaves, buds, and grasshoppers. At such times the hunter, by piping seductive quavers, may tickle his vanity and stir anew his passion, when he will stop in his hunt for food and commence to gobble, strut, and gyrate enough to exhaust your patience, but if you call properly and are cool and quiet he will come.

The turkey's gobble is easily heard at a distance of from one to two miles if the air is still and clear.

These are the rules that apply to turkeys in general, but there are exceptions; for instance, some old gobblers never secure the favor of even one hen during the whole season, but will run and prowl the country over, seeking such stray females as may be met with, even visiting the grangers' domestic flocks, which is not an unfrequent circumstance in settled neighborhoods. These solitary old birds when met with are easy prey to the expert caller.

CHAPTER XII
ON CALLERS AND CALLING

There are in use by all hunters who still-hunt the turkey, instruments used for imitating the call-notes of this bird; a few lines on these useful implements will not be amiss here.

The box or trough call, the splinter and slate, the leaf call, all have their merits, and can be made to imitate the different notes of the hens and young gobblers. The leaf call is simply a tender leaf from particular trees, held between the lips, and when well executed, the call with it is good. The box call is said to make excellent imitation of the hen call, but I have yet to see one that satisfied me. The box call is made by taking a piece of wood, preferably poplar, or some other soft wood, about four inches long, two inches deep, by one and a quarter thick. Mortise a square hole in this block, leaving the ends one half inch thick, one side one eighth, the other quite thin. The mortise is one and a half inches deep. A piece of slate some four inches long by half an inch wide is drawn across the thin edge of this box in various positions, and one skilled in the use of this call can obtain very good results. The call most in use by the backwoods turkey hunters in the Southern States, and one that causes the death of more turkeys than all other call devices put together, is simply the hollow wing bone from the second joint of a hen turkey, with both ends cut off to allow free passage of air. One end is held with the lips in such a manner that the inside portion of the lips covers the end of the bone. The breath is then drawn in sharply, and when one is skilled in its use the different call-notes of the hen turkey can be produced perfectly. There are several other devices much after this order, but I have never found use for any of them; in fact their defects prompted me to invent a call of my own, which I prefer. First, get the smaller bone from the wing of a wild hen turkey: the radius of the forearm. Hallock says the larger bone, but he is wrong. The bone should be thoroughly cleansed of all its marrow. After cutting off nearly one half inch from each end of the bone, the ends are made quite smooth with a file, all rough surface removed, and the bone finished with fine sandpaper or emery. The round end of this bone is packed and glued into the end of a piece of reed cane joint two inches long and three-eighths in diameter. Then a nice nickel-plated ferrule or thimble is fitted on the cane to prevent splitting, and the sloping end is wrapped with silk. Next, get another joint of cane that the first piece will just fit into and glue them tightly together; then cut off until the right tone is produced. The flat end of the bone is used as the mouth-piece. The end of the bone that is inserted in the cane is wrapped with tissue paper wet with glue and pushed firmly into the cane three quarters of an inch, and care must be taken to make this call air-tight at the joints; when the glue dries, it will be strong, air-tight, and durable. The bands or ferrules are intended to make the instrument doubly strong, as well as to improve its looks. It is a tedious job to make a good call, but when you have one properly made, it will last a great while, and I think this particular call is the best in the world.

JORDAN'S TURKEY CALL

There is one objection to the box, slate, or similar calls: they make quite a noise near by but can not be heard any distance. The instrument I make can be heard a half or three quarters of a mile away.

This call is used by taking the flat bone end between the lips and by measured sucking motion the notes are produced. The cluck is produced by placing the tip of the tongue on the end of the mouth-piece, and giving a sudden jerk and suck. This, according to my opinion, is the most natural cluck that was ever made by any instrument, and it can be modulated so as to seduce or alarm at the will of the operator.

It is necessary to practise the use of a caller until proficiency is attained, the same as you would do in playing a flute or violin. Calling, in my opinion, is the most important thing to be considered when in quest of the turkey, and the knowledge of how to do it is difficult to impart to others.

There are four distinct calls of the wild turkey one should become familiar with to become an expert turkey hunter; these are the call of the young hen, the old hen, the young gobbler, and the gobble of the old male bird. The latter is almost impossible to learn, and I have seen but two or three men in my life who could imitate the gobble. The sound is made with the throat, and I know of no way it can be taught. The notes of the hen turkey consist of a variety of quavering sounds such as are given by the domestic fowl, but which require study and practice, with the best devised caller, to imitate. The plain yelp or "*keow-keow*" are the chief notes to learn, and once mastered and employed in concert with the cluck, will usually be all that is necessary in calling turkey, be it a flock of scattered individuals or an old gobbler (in the gobbling season), but it would avail nothing on the latter at any other time. "*Keow-keow-keow*," or "*keow-kee-kee*," "*cut*," "*cut*"—these are the variety of notes, and each has its meaning, however singular that may appear. The turkey has no song, and the notes it employs are either conversational, call, distress, or alarm notes.

Early morning, when they are dropping down from their roost, is the best time to study their language as well as their habits. If you go near a flock of tame turkeys and begin to yelp and cluck, they will reply and keep it up as long as you do, so you can soon learn their language. If the turkeys be wild ones, keep well out of sight, for they will stand no familiarity. I am not, however, a stickler about keeping out of sight when calling. I prefer to sit in front of a tree that is on the side from which the turkey is expected to approach, rather than to get behind it. I sit in front of the tree in such a manner that a turkey with the keenest eye in the world will not identify me, if properly fixed, clothed, and motionless. The explanation of this is that the gobbler is not looking for a person, but for another turkey; and as it can think of but one thing at a time, it sees nothing that does not resemble that which it is in quest of; but if you move, its keen eye will quickly detect you.

The turkeys seem to have no special power of smell, so if the hunter's clothes are gray or drab, he may sit at the base of a tree, and by keeping quiet, the turkey will many times come within ten or twenty feet, and, although looking directly at him, will fail to make him out and walk leisurely away.

I once had a flock of wild turkeys come very near me, and some of them jumped up and stood on the log I was resting my back against; one hen was within three feet of me, and she stood for a few minutes purring and looking me over, finally leaping off. Then a young gobbler came in front and took a good look at me. He seemed to have a suspicion that I was not a stump, for he walked back a little and stopped to meditate. Not being satisfied with his first investigation, he came up again and took a better look; after satisfying himself he walked leisurely away. He looked so quizzically at me that I could scarcely refrain from laughing. At the same time these inquisitive birds were looking me over, my rifle was trained on an immense gobbler within eighty yards strutting in plain view. Upon him my attention was chiefly fastened, and in a few minutes the old fellow came to bag. A dead grass colored suit is not so good for a turkey hunting suit as one gray or brown.

If the game you seek be an old gobbler, and the time spring, you will employ the call fully as much as when calling the scattered brood in fall or winter. I generally use the plain, quaint, easy measured yelp or quaver and cluck of the female; this same call has a hundred variations, but it is not necessary that you employ all of them. The simple "cluck-cluck-cluck" and now and then plain "keow-keow," when properly done, is generally effective. I have called as loud as I could, so as to be heard a mile away, while an old gobbler was standing near enough for me to see the light of his eyes without alarming him. Again I have called very low, just as a test, with the same result. Sometimes the old bird is unusually cautious; then the less calling the better; then, after you have engaged the attention of the turkey so that it will stop and gobble and strut, the less you call him the better, for the reason that in gobbling and strutting it is using all its own persuasive power to draw you to him, thinking you are a hen. Under these conditions so long as you continue to call or reply he will remain and gobble, and insist on your coming to him. But if you have commanded his attention and stop calling and wait, he will make up his mind to come to you, as he has come to the conclusion that the hen is indifferent to his company and is moving away from him; this will excite his anxiety and cause him to make haste toward you.

Under such circumstances, and they occur very often, the hunter will very soon note, after he has quit calling, the gobbler will gobble oftener, more furiously, and strut with greater vigor. This is the time when most turkey hunters make a fatal mistake, for if you call after the gobbler starts toward you, he will stop a while at that point, and go through all the maneuvers he has been worrying you with for some time, march back and

94

forth to his recent stand and give you another hour or two of waiting, or perhaps he will go away to return no more. Do not make this mistake, but keep still, wait, and watch. Let the gobbler do the gobbling and strutting, and you do nothing but keep your eye on your rifle sights and watch for his appearance. When he suddenly stops gobbling and strutting look sharp and keep your gun leveled in the direction from which he is expected, but by no means have your gun in such a position that you will have to move it after the turkey is in sight. Some men have a habit of moving their guns about, although they have their heads and bodies hidden and quiet. They might as well get up and say "hello."

I soon saw the old gobbler stealing slowly through the brush

If a gobbler stops, and gobbles and struts in one place some time, while you are calling him, this is good evidence that he will come to you, if you have but patience and keep quiet; nine hunters out of ten, however, take the opposite view of it, and for the lack of good understanding of the turkey, and of patience, get up and go home at the very time when success would have crowned their efforts. Now, if a hen has gone to the gobbler, as will often occur, and they are out of your sight in the brush, you will know this to be the case by the long interval between gobbles; if it be fifteen to twenty minutes, you may be certain a hen is with him.

You cannot always be sure that a cessation of gobbling is for the purpose of attending the hen or of coming to you, but you will soon find out if you wait, as the turkey is sure to strut and gobble near the place after the caress is over; this has been my experience hundreds of times; in fact it is characteristic and habitual, and it rarely happens otherwise. Here is an instance: Two young men accompanied me once to a creek near the margin of a large prairie in Texas to see me call an old gobbler. At the dawn of day the gobbler broke forth into a lively gobbling, when we proceeded to an old fallen pine log to call him. Having waited for him to fly down from his roost, I began the regulation series of calls, clucks, etc. The turkey was a great gobbler and did his share of it, but he would not come immediately to the call. After a while one of the boys remarked that he heard a hen yelping near the gobbler, and then all gobbling ceased, and the boys remarked he had gone off with the hen. I said, "No, he is there yet." This silence lasted fifteen or twenty minutes, while the mosquitoes were covering the faces of the boys; but they were bent on seeing the play out and would squirm and rub off the pests, then listen and look, as they lay prone on the pine straw and peered over the log. Once in a while I would yelp, but no response came until the gobbler's attention to the hen had ceased; he then began to gobble again as vigorously as though nothing had occurred. Then I began calling again, but he would not come to me, and soon another hen came flying and lighted in a tree near him, and a moment or two after flew down to him. This caused another long wait. When through with the second hen there was another long strutting and then another hen paid him a visit. By this time the boys had become impatient, and were anxious to go home; the mosquitoes were biting them severely and their stomachs were craving nourishment; so was mine, but I knew what I was about, and in a low whisper remarked: "Boys, if you can endure it no longer we will go home, but it is hard to have come this far before daylight, six miles, and have such a fine gobbler within our grasp, then give it up and go home without him."

"Oh, well," both said in a whisper, "if you think you will get him, we will stay all day."

"That is all I ask," I replied. "On these terms he goes home with us."

By this time the gobbler had finished his attention to the third hen and was gobbling furiously in the same spot. I began to call again and the gobbler responded lustily. Having given him a few well-meant calls, I put the caller in my pocket. Seeing this move, one of the boys asked me if I was going to give up. "No," I replied, "it is his turn to parley and he will come now if no other hen comes to him, so you fellows keep still as death, but keep a careful watch."

Very soon, after a series of rapid and excited gobbling, all was still. My rifle got into position, and I whispered to the boys to peer over the log, but to keep their heads still, as the gobbler was coming and would soon be in sight. The woods had been burned and the low scrub in our region was black and charred, save small spots that had escaped the fire. I soon saw the white top of the old gobbler's head stealing slowly through the dead brush a hundred yards away, but the boys could not see him until he walked upon a small mound some three feet in height, that brought his whole form above the dead bushes. His feathers were all down, lying close to his body, and his long beard hung low; a noble bird he was. The most thrilling and picturesque object to my eye is the long beard of the turkey; just as the big horns of a buck are to the deer hunter. In a low whisper I asked the boys if they saw him. "Yes, yes," both answered in a trembling whisper. Then the rifle cracked and the bird sprang into the air and fell back dead. The two boys, wild with delight, sprang to their feet and went crashing through the burned underbrush to get hold of the fallen turkey. One of the young men, quite a hunter, remarked: "That beats all the maneuvering with a gobbler I have ever seen and was well worth the long ride to witness." So presenting him with the big twenty-two pound bird, we went home.

As soon as possible select a place to call from. To a novice there is no special rule by which one can at all times be governed in calling old gobblers. Each bird is possessed of some peculiarity different from its neighbor, and all individual variations the hunter must meet with good judgment. When out very early in the morning in the vicinity of turkeys, get some elevated position, a ridge if possible, and, as the dawn is breaking, listen for the gobble. The first sounds one is apt to hear are the hooting of the owls; the next, as the light grows apace, is the note of the cardinal, found in all southern woodlands. As a roseate glow begins to replace the gray dawn, one will hear the "*gil-obble-obble-obble*." It may be within one hundred yards of you or perhaps a mile away. You should wait until the turkey gobbles again to be certain of his direction, then make all haste to him, and get as near as you wish before he flies down from his roost. When within one hundred and fifty yards of the gobbler, stop, and be careful lest he sees you, as his ever watchful eyes look everywhere, especially at things on the ground.

As soon as possible select a place to call from. To a novice an old treetop or log is best, but to me the front of a tree is preferable, with an open space in front that the gobbler may come into to be shot. But whatever the place selected, get into position as soon as possible, and let it always be an attitude that will not cramp you should you have to remain a long time, and where you can have easy action for your arms and gun. That is why I prefer the side of a tree next to the game.

If the gobbler is still gobbling after you have seated yourself, sit quietly until he flies down; that is best. But if you cluck or yelp to him in the tree, let it be but once or twice to attract attention and no more; no matter how much he gobbles, you must keep still until he leaves his roost, and even then wait a few moments for him to gobble or strut, which he is sure to do on reaching the ground, after taking a look around. After this you can give him a cluck or yelp, or several of them, no matter how many, provided they

98

are well delivered. If you are not yet an expert at calling, best make as few calls as possible; for he will surely reply by either gobbling or strutting, or both. Do not be in a hurry, for generally he is in no hurry, but has all day to worry you, and will surely do it if you continue calling after you have said enough. If you desire to get your shot at the gobbler as early as possible, call as little as you can after you have got him interested. If you continue to yelp every time he gobbles, he will stop in one place and gobble anywhere from two to six hours, exhausting all your patience and temper.

In selecting a place to call from, there is one caution that should never be forgotten: never get behind a tree so that you will have to look from one side to point the gun; the turkey is sure to see you and run away before you can shoot.

CHAPTER XIII
CALLING UP THE LOVELORN GOBBLER

There is a wide difference between the old gobbler and the young gobbler, and the tactics to be employed in hunting them are quite different. At two years old he can be distinguished by his beard, which is then about five inches in length, the tip having a burned appearance; his spurs are about five eighths of an inch long, are not pointed, while the average weight of the bird is about sixteen to eighteen pounds. At three years this burned appearance disappears and the beard is seven or eight inches long, straight, black, and glossy, the spurs being an inch or more and pointed. The bird may now be considered full grown, and weighs from nineteen to twenty-two pounds. Henceforth there is no way I know of to tell his age. He continues to grow for several years, taking on fat as he gets older, while the beard will attain to a length of twelve to thirteen inches, when it wears off at the tip on account of dragging on the ground while the bird feeds. But the beard does not indicate the size of the turkey, as some very small gobblers have extremely long ones. The largest turkey I ever saw had an eight-inch beard and weighed twenty-four pounds even though quite lean; he would have weighed thirty-one or thirty-three pounds if he had been fat, and he may have been twenty years old, for he was known to have inhabited one locality for more than fifteen years.

You must first ascertain where the gobblers are to be found, and then be on the ground before there is the least sign of daybreak to select a place where you can sit hidden and in comfort. If satisfied that gobblers are in the vicinity, wait until dawn approaches, and if then you do not hear them, hoot like the barred owl. If there is an old gobbler within hearing, nine times out of ten he will gobble when the owl hoots; but if you get no response, "owl" again, or give a low cluck; the old gobbler may be on his roost within sight of you. If still no response, cluck louder, and repeat at intervals, adding a few short, spirited yelps; if you fail, move quickly a half or quarter mile away and call loudly with a cluck and yelp or two. Proceed in this manner until you have traversed the range of your proposed hunt. In this way I have encountered several old gobblers in a morning's tramp, while there was not one within hearing of the point first selected.

If turkeys have begun gobbling at dawn, you must choose a place to call from. My choice is in front of a tree a little larger than one's body, facing the turkey. If possible have your back to a thicket with open ground in front, or you may prefer to get behind a log or stump, or in a fallen treetop. Do not make a blind, for the obstruction will hide the game which is as apt to approach from one direction as another; generally the unexpected way. If you sit out in an open place by a tree, and stick up two or three short bushes in front, he will never see you until near enough for you to shoot.

If the old gobbler is in the tree before you take your position, do not approach nearer than one hundred to one hundred and fifty yards of him; he may possibly see you or he may fly behind you, or alight at your side when you call, and run away before you can shoot. This may look like a small matter to consider, but you will find it amounts to much in dealing with old gobblers, as I have learned from experience. I have had them fly right over my head, so close that I could have touched them with my gun barrel, or alight at my side and run away in a twinkling. One flew so near my brother once as to flip his hat brim with its wing. The most remarkable instance I ever knew occurred to a Mr. Daughty in Alabama. He was calling a turkey that was gobbling in a tall pine, and finding the call would not bring him down, Mr. Daughty took off his old brown felt hat and gave it a flop or two over his knees. Before he had time to think the gobbler was upon him, and he had to drop his gun and ward it off with his hands. He told me the gobbler had stretched out his feet to alight on his head and frightened him so he never thought of his gun, and was so dazed that the gobbler was gone before he recovered his wits. I once called one down, and as he stretched his legs to alight, he saw me, and with a loud "*put-put*," checked his flight and shot up like a rocket.

A gobbler will invariably alight within fifty to seventy-five yards of the roosting tree, according to the height they are perched from the ground; therefore one hundred and fifty yards is sufficiently near if your purpose is to call; but if you intend to stalk and shoot him in the tree, you will do best if you show no part of your body; and especially keep the gun barrel out of sight. Many hunters will hide themselves but expose their gun, which is a great mistake, as the bird will surely see the glint of light on the barrel.

It is best, in my opinion, not to call while the gobblers are in the trees, for the reason that the gobbler is expecting the hen to come to him; and it will often happen that as long as you call, so long will he remain in the tree and gobble and strut. I have had gobblers sit on their roost until 9 o'clock and gobble because I kept yelping.

"Cluck," "put," "put," there stands a gobbler, within twenty paces to the left; he has approached from the rear

Having got into position, wait until your nerves are cool. The turkey hunter must have time. Give a low, soothing cluck, then listen carefully, as the turkey may gobble the instant he hears the cluck; perhaps two may answer, but we will confine our attention to one. If a two-year-old bird, he will gobble before he thinks; but we will not allow you such an easy job as a two-year-old. Suppose the gobbler is three years or over—he will straighten up his long neck and listen some moments. He is not sure it was a genuine cluck, but he thinks it was, and duly drops his broad wings, partly spreads his tail, and listens; then, "*Vut-v-r-r-o-o-o-m-m-i*" comes the booming strut, and "*Gil-obble-obble-obble*," if he dares this it is to elicit a call or cluck from you to make sure he is not deceived. Now call, "*Cluck, cluck, keow, keow, keow*," at once he answers "*Gil-obble-obble-obble*" two or three times in a breath so loud and shrill that it rings out like thunder in the quiet of the forest. Now give a low quaver, "*Keow, keow, keow*," just audible to him, yet low, then stop right there. He will yell out in a fierce and prolonged rattle that will make the squirrels quit their feeding and spring to the trunk of the tree, and arouse the herons from the margin of the rivers and swamp ponds. Then comes the heavy booming strut, and if he gobbles again, be quiet and let him talk to his heart's content. Unless you yelp or cluck at this time, he becomes more and more nervous and restless, and even dances on the limb. Keep quiet; he will now give a few lusty gobbles, and then there is a short pause. Look out now. There is a rustle in the tree, a flip, flip, and you see his big dark form leave the tree and sail to the ground, giving his broad wings a flop or two to ease up the impetus, and as he strikes the earth a cloud of leaves arise in a circle to settle around him. The royal bird straightens up his matchless form, and while his fine hazel eyes scan the surroundings, you gaze with admiration at his symmetry and beauty. More likely than not he has alighted to one side; if so, beware! Probably, too, if the woods are not very open, you will not see him on the ground and must judge as to his movements.

If there be but one gobbler, wait a few minutes after he is down, as he is listening and watching; then make a few yelps softly, but rapidly, and a cluck or two. He will gobble and strut vehemently. Be sure your cluck is a perfect assembly cluck, or he may take it as an alarm "*put*." Your cluck, if made at all, should have a reassuring accent, or better not attempt it, depending on the yelp or quaver. The cluck and "*put*" are so nearly similar in sound to the ear that they are difficult to distinguish; but one is a call note and the other is an alarm, hence it were better to omit both rather than disturb the confidence of the bird you are calling. While the two notes are impossible to describe in words, they can readily be produced by an expert caller with a good instrument. Give the gobbler two or three quick little yelps, "*Keow, keow, kee, kee,*" in a kind of an interrogatory tone; this is sure to make him gobble and strut, or probably to strut only. I prefer that he strut, although the gobble is more exhilarating to one's ear, but does not signify as much. The strut is the better sign every time; it shows he has leisure and passion.

Your "*Cluck, keow, ku-ku,*" brings forth at once "*Gil-obble-obble-obble. Cluck-v-r r-o-o-o-mi.*" Hush, hear that? "*Cut-o-r-r-r,*" "*Cut, cut keow, keow, keow.*" What is it? Is some one else calling? No; the sound is too perfect. Hark! how he gobbles and struts with renewed vigor, for it is the siren note of the real hen who has gone to him. You might as well now keep quiet for fifteen or twenty minutes, for he will not answer as long as he is with a hen. As soon as she is out of sight, however, he will listen to you. Here, reader, is the most important lesson to be learned and the most valuable in all turkey lore—patience.

Suddenly there was a "Gil-obble-obble-obble," so near it made

me jump, and there within twenty paces of me was the gobbler

Fifteen minutes is usually ample time with the lusty turkey. You keep up the call and tease at proper intervals until sufficient zeal is restored, which can be determined by the vigor of his gobble; then do not call any more, no matter what he does. Keep still and watch his manœuvres, and presently he will begin to gobble and strut with great stress, gyrate, and swerve from side to side, right to left, his big tail, doing everything to fetch the new hen whose voice he hears; but you must not break the spell by any false move. All at once he stops and everything is still again. Maybe another hen has come to his court, maybe not. But do not yelp or cluck; he may be coming to you, for he knows precisely where you are, and if he is not caressing another hen he is surely approaching you. This may take fully an hour, sometimes six.

"*Cluck, put, put,*" there stands a young gobbler within twenty paces to the left: he has approached from the rear. Make no motion. He has not identified you. "*Put, put.*" Keep still. "*Put, o-r-r-r.*" He begins to step high, turning to one side, then to the other. "*C-r-r-r.*" He pulls out the tip of one wing and places it on the other. Note that. He is going to walk away. "*Put, c-r-r-r.*" He is gone; but let him go, and good riddance, for he has created a distrust in the old gobbler's mind that will take some time to remove. You are now compelled to change your place and call again. "*Gil-obble-obble-obble.*" Gracious! he is off to the right and fifty yards nearer. If there is sufficient cover, make a detour of from one hundred and fifty to two hundred yards and get ahead of him; then sit down, give a yelp or two, and end with a cluck. That will reassure him at once, and he will most surely gobble in reply; if so, you sit still. Have your rifle in readiness so that no move be made when he comes into view. Very likely you have waited some time since he gobbled last, and apparently he has quit all strutting. There is another ominous pause, but you are ready for him and on the sharp lookout. You are sorely vexed, but your good judgment keeps you alert while the other hunters have long since gone home.

"*Gil-obble-obble-obble.*" Sh-e-e-e-e. There he is within thirty paces to the right at a half strut. What a bird! See his noble bearing, the bronzed coat, the

104

glint in the keen eye. You can't move now, for he sees you, but he has not made you out. Be still and let him pass behind that big oak, then turn quickly before he comes into view again. Ah! that low green bush has obscured him; he has passed out of sight and does not reappear. Your nerves begin to run like the wheels of a clock with the balance off. Your disappointment is inconsolable. "*Gil-obble-obble-obble*," nearly one hundred yards on his way. This is discouraging, but the educated turkey hunter never gives up so long as a gobbler will argue with him.

Get up at once and make a rapid detour, taking in two hundred yards; get ahead of him again and on his line of march. Then sit down and call as soon as possible to attract his attention. This done your chances are as good as ever. "*Gil-obble-obble-obble*." You have estimated well. The gobbler is one hundred yards back yet, which gives you a breathing spell. He begins to rehearse the old rôle of gobbling and strutting, but with greater force, as he has had a long rest. Now give another call and cluck to see where he is; no response, and you are becoming as restless as a raccoon robbing a yellow-jacket's nest, and crazy for just one more call; but I advise not; have patience, and wait. Another call would only cause delay if not other harm. He is the one now to get nervous, for that hen may escape. A crow gives a sudden caw in a neighboring tree, and, "*Gil-obble-obble-obble*," says the turkey, now only seventy-five yards away. But you are silent. Again comes a long pause, and you think he has detected you and gone. A red tail hawk darts screaming through the timber, and, "*Gil-obble-obble-obble cluck v-r-r-o-o-m-i*," goes your bird thirty yards nearer; then all is silent again. He has made a strenuous effort to draw your call, but you are deaf. Another long pause and you are in a tremor all over. He has quit making any noise, and the stillness is painful for, save a solitary red bird trilling his carol in yon elm, and a gray squirrel nibbling the buds on that slender maple, all is still. Two chameleons are racing on the log behind which you are crouching, and, springing suddenly to the dry leaves, they startle you with the clattering they make, so highly strung are your nerves; but you dare not move.

Why this insufferable silence? The gobbler is coming, but when will he appear? Your rifle is in position, cocked, your eye running along the glistening barrel, but that is all of you which is allowed to move. A distant dead tree falls with a heavy thud that shakes the earth. "*Gil-obble-obble-obble*," breaks upon your ear and sends a thrill through your nerves, and the timid squirrel wiggling and scampering to his hole in a hollow gum. The sound comes from the oblique left. Your eyes turn slowly that way. Ah! there he stands, half erect, half concealed in the brush. You see the white top of his head, the crimson wattles of his arched neck, the long beard and the glint of his eye, for he is only forty paces away; but do not fire, as the least twig may deflect the ball. He has not made you out, although in plain view, nor will he, unless you make a sudden move.

You have carefully brought the rifle to bear on him. He is meditative and somewhat listless; but note that tail going up: he is going to strut, and that will bring him into an open space. "*Cluck v-r-r-o-o-o-m-i.*" There! he is broadside on. See that crease that runs along his neck ending near the butt of the wing? Drop your bead on the butt of the wing opposite where that crease ends. That will kill him every time, as behind lies his heart; while if you aim for the centre of the body the bullet will go through the viscera, making a mess of it, and while a fatal wound, he may get away and be lost to you, for it will not always knock him down. If he stands quartering, aim at the centre of the breast next to you. It will at once be fatal. If the back is presented, which is not once in a hundred times, draw upon the centre of it. Unless turkeys are very plentiful, and you care little about losing a good chance, don't shoot at his head with a rifle.

CHAPTER XIV
THE INDIFFERENT YOUNG GOBBLER

Of all stages, conditions, and peculiarities of these fowls, the young gobbler is the most difficult to understand. He is absolutely unique, hence you must employ entirely different tactics when you go in quest of him. He has little education, but he possesses a great native shrewdness, and I have sometimes thought him more difficult to get than either the old gobbler or hen; this may be a fool's luck, or it may be the result of stupidity or reticence, but I have killed ten old gobblers to one young one. As I have before stated, while the young males are with their mothers and sisters in the flock there is little difficulty in bringing them to the call after the flock is scattered. But after the separation of the sexes they are extremely hard to call, for the reason that they have abandoned the society of the females altogether, and do not pay any attention to their voices. Lack of information and a reckless carelessness have caused the loss of many young gobblers that otherwise might have been secured. After the young males have been separated some time from the females, and are banded together, they are hard to find and hard to bag when found. Instead of flushing at once into the tree at the approach of an enemy, they usually take to their legs and run some distance before stopping, making their pursuit difficult and unreliable. If once flushed and scattered, and the hunter understands how to call them, he can usually get one or two out of the flock if he is familiar with their peculiar ways. Thus after December we have three distinct classes of turkey society, the old gobblers, the young gobblers, and the hens; and no matter what the number of them is, they persistently maintain this separation the rest of the winter.

The soft, gentle quaver of the hen has no effect on the ear of the young gobbler at this season, and he will hearken to no other note or call than that of the young gobbler. Even were a flock of hens to pass beneath the tree on which he is perched, he would regard them with no more interest than he would a flock of crows; hence neither the hen nor her yelp would be a decoy to him, but the call of another young gobbler will enlist his attention. The call of the young gobbler, like that of the average boy as he is developing into manhood, is changeable and erratic; at times it is ridiculous from its awkwardness, and hard to imitate or even to identify. It consists of an irregular hoarse and discordant croak and a coarse muffled cluck that sounds like an acorn falling into a pool of water, or the gentle tap of a stick on a log. If this yelp or cluck is properly and timely made, it will bring the young gobbler to the hunter, but usually he is in no haste to come even then. They have ample time to spare for all their movements, and it requires the greatest patience and dogged determination of which a sportsman is capable to sit and wait their pleasure; but if the hunter has a band of young gobblers well scattered, if he has a good caller and is expert in its use, and will make up his mind to sit quiet and talk turkey, he will usually be rewarded. He should use only one or two low, coarse clucks, well measured and some time apart; then the low, muffled "*Croc, croc.*" The young gobbler may be sitting on the limb of a tall cypress, hidden from view by a festoon of Spanish moss; or, if in a pine, hidden by the limbs, as still as a part of the tree. "*Croc, croc,*" and one low, hoarse cluck, as if a nut had struck the bark of a dead log in falling, are the only sounds you dare to make. He is not so reckless in regard to the call or answers as the hens, and not so nervous. While he sits and contemplates, he measures notes; so that you have to be careful if you would fool him. Now call, "*Croc, croc.*" His fears begin to dissipate, and running his beak through his feathers, he makes his toilet. This over, he slowly raises his long neck and head and replies, "*Croc, croc.*" "*Cong, cong, croc, croc, cluck.*" He turns his head with one side earthward, and gives himself a convulsive shake—"*Croc, croc.*" He lifts up one foot and then slowly puts it down; lifts one wing, placing its tip on top of the other, then slips that one out and laps it on the first. "*Croc, croc, kee, kee.*" He looks around again to be reassured. Now there is a rustle in the top of the tree, and you see the leaves move, for he has turned on the limb and you may see a portion of his body. You dare not shoot or risk a bullet through that brush. Wait. "*Croc, croc*"; he walks along the limb a few feet, but you still get only glimpses. "*Croc, croc,*" and down he sails to the earth. A cloud of dry leaves arises around him and settles again as he closes his broad wings and straightens up. Now is your chance; bag him.

The soft, gentle quaver of the hen has no effect on the ear of the

young gobbler

When the young gobbler once makes up his mind to go to your call, there is little or no stopping on his part. He walks boldly along, as if he had no fear of anything. But be careful; he will see you surely if you make an unnecessary motion, and there is no compromising a mistake with him. His adieu is final. He is a bird of the fewest words at any time, and stands upon the idea that absolute silence is safety. His habits are exclusive and retiring, seldom showing himself in openings, although at times he is fond of open pastures or prairies where he can see all around him.

CHAPTER XV
HUNTING TURKEY WITH A DOG

I do not believe there is any safer way of bringing a turkey to bag than by the judicious employment of a good turkey dog, and by that I mean a dog trained especially to hunt turkeys. The hunter, too, who employs a dog must know and act his part well to be successful.

Of all times to hunt the wild turkey with a dog, the autumn and winter months are the best. The dog should be a natural bird dog, either pointer or setter. My choice, next to the pointers or setters, are the terriers, either Scotch or fox. The Scotch terrier makes an excellent turkey dog, due to its intelligence, patience, courage, and snap.

I have had dogs lie by my side when turkeys were gobbling and strutting within a few feet, and never move a muscle until the gun was fired, when they would be upon the bird instantly.

If you employ a dog in gobbling time, he must be thoroughly educated to distinctly know his part, which is to keep at heel or lie at your side and watch without a sound until the bird is called to gun and shot; then the dog is allowed to go and seize the quarry if it is not killed by the shot and making off with a broken wing.

In Alabama I once saw a large gobbler coming slowly to my call over a pine hill about ninety yards away. I fired at him with my rifle as he was moving in a full strut. At the shot, my gobbler tumbled over, but quickly got up and made off at a lively run with one wing hanging. I started after him, at the same time calling to my brother (who was below me on a creek, calling another turkey) to let go his dog. In a moment I saw a gray streak shoot out from the thicket on the creek, and start up the hill in pursuit of the running gobbler. It was my brother's Scotch terrier, and within one hundred and fifty yards the dog overhauled the gobbler, to my great satisfaction, and held him until I arrived. Had I not had the services of a dog at this time the turkey would have escaped, as he could get up the high, rocky slope faster than I.

It is best to take a young dog six or eight months old. The training is easy enough, provided the preceptor knows his part. Like educating a dog for quail, he must get the rudiments before he ever sees the live game, for once a lesson is spoiled a dog is also spoiled. Give him a few lessons before taking him into the woods to hunt turkeys. He must know the turkey is his quest ere he is let loose; and do not loose him until you have found unmistakably fresh signs; for one mistake at such a time will take months to repair.

Teach him to lie down, the same as in quail lessons, no matter if he is a pointer, terrier, or hound. Having taught him to lie down, take him walking where there are trees, logs, and fences, and every now and then suddenly sit or squat down by some tree or fence, calling him quickly to you by soft words and motion of the hand. Make him lie down close to your hip, better the left side if you are right handed, so that by any unexpected move he may not destroy your aim at a critical moment. Teach him to lie on his belly or with his head prone between his forepaws. This is easily done, and will insure a motionless attitude as a turkey is approaching. If he whines under excitement, as some will, tap him lightly with a small switch on the head; this will also make him put his head down, and he will soon understand the meaning of it.

Next get a dead wild turkey, hen if possible, as it is lighter. Take the dog into the yard or field where there are no dogs or children to bother him. Let him play with the turkey a little, while you encourage him, then have some one drag the turkey from him by the head a short distance, while you hold and encourage the dog to go. Let the turkey be hung up in a tree or bush out of his reach; then let him go and take the trail and tree the bird, and encourage him to bark and jump against the tree. Then have it fixed so that after he has jumped and barked a while you can fire a gun or pistol and the carcass falls to the ground and he pounces upon it. Repeat this as often as you have an opportunity. You may keep a wing cut off at the second joint, using that for several lessons before it becomes tainted, but by no means allow him to tear the wing or bite the flesh of the turkey. You might set him after a tame turkey now and then, but this might bring him some day to grief by a load of shot from your good neighbor.

Take the dog with you on a few hunts in the woods for turkeys. If you find a flock, put him after them at once and let him flush them, which he will hardly fail to do. Then, if you can kill one over him, your turkey dog is well-nigh made. Having had your turkeys flushed, you can walk slowly and cautiously in the direction they flew, looking into every tree, and you will soon see one or two of them perched upon a limb. To get your bird now is easy if you have a good rifle; and you had better not be out if you haven't one, as no kind of shooting requires better marksmanship than turkey shooting, especially in the timber. Having treed your turkey, you may get several shots, and meantime the dog is allowed to trot around and bark as he sees fit, as the more noise he makes the more is the attention of the birds diverted from you to him; but after you have looked among the trees in a few hundred yards of the flush, if you have not secured your bird, select a good place to call. Sit down with your back against a tree, or behind a log or fallen tree if that suits you better. Sit quite flat and low, bringing the knees nearly up to the eyes. Call the dog to you at once by a whisper and wave of the hand, and make him lie snugly at your side, looking in the direction you look.

After a few minutes, when everything is still, you begin to call at short intervals. Now and then a low yelp, at first, and if you get a reply, cease calling until the results begin to show up, either by one or more turkeys coming to your call, or in their collecting together in another direction, which is more likely to be the case, from the fact that the mother hen is doing more effective calling than you, or they are inclined to go that way anyhow. In such a case you must get up at once and proceed in the direction you see them flying. Go quickly to where they are collecting. Put the dog after them again and into the trees they will go; you then proceed as at first and continue these tactics until you have got what you want, or have lost them entirely.

This is excellent and exciting sport, and the dog loves it and soon becomes an expert in the chase. But of all methods of hunting the turkey it is the most disastrous, next to baiting, not so much in the number of birds killed, but the turkey has a great dread of a dog, and if too frequently chased by one it will drive the birds out of the locality. It should seldom be practised in the same locality or upon the same flock of turkeys more than once in a season.

The rifle is preëminently the gun to employ in this method of

112

hunting, and there is a great satisfaction in taking a fine bird from its lofty perch in a tall pine, gum, or cypress at one hundred to one hundred and fifty yards, where it would be safe from any shotgun.

Dogs trained to hunt turkeys must not be allowed to run squirrels, hares, deer, or any woodland game. It makes no difference as to quail or prairie game, but in the timber his work belongs to the turkey alone.

In teaching the young dog to grasp a turkey, it should be trained to seize the bird by the neck every time, and not touch the body, as his teeth will lacerate the tender skin and tear the flesh—a thing no true sportsman would tolerate. It is easy to teach the dog not to mouth the game by making him take the neck in his mouth every time an opportunity is afforded. If he takes hold of the body, or mouths the feathers, make him let go and take the neck. He will soon learn this.

The common fox hound also makes a good turkey dog, and takes naturally to it, but he is too noisy. A turkey dog must not yelp or bark on the track before he sees the birds as the hound does. Turkeys are alarmed easily and prefer to run instead of to fly, and if the dog barks on the trail they will run for miles, all the time probably not one hundred yards in advance of the dog. So the dog for turkeys must keep silent until in sight of them, and then bark savagely until they are all flushed. This the pointer, setter, or terrier will do. Be sure to encourage your dog to bark at the turkeys in the trees.

Audubon says: "In the spring when the males are much emaciated by their attention to the hens, it sometimes happens that, in plain, open ground they may be overtaken by a swift dog, in which case they squat and allow themselves to be seized, either by the dog or the hunter, who has followed on a good horse." I have heard of such occurrences, but I never saw an instance of the kind. Good dogs scent the turkeys when in large flocks at a great distance; I may venture to say half a mile away, if the wind is right. Should the dog be well trained to the sport, he will set off at full speed on getting the scent and in silence until he sees the birds, when he instantly barks, and, running among them, forces the whole flock to take to the trees in different directions. This is of great advantage to the hunter, for, should all the turkeys go one way, they would soon leave the perches and run again; but when they are separated by the dog, a person accustomed to the sport finds the birds easily and shoots them at pleasure.

No turkey is going to run very long ahead of a dog, if the dog is in sight and chasing him. A pack of mouthy beagles, or an old, slow deer-hound, giving mouth continually, might keep a turkey in a trot until fatigued; it is possible then that a quick, swift dog like the Scotch terrier or the pointer might rush on and catch him. But the first impulse of the turkey, on the near approach of an enemy, is to fly and not to depend on its legs; though on seeing an enemy at some distance, turkeys will run away and not fly at all.

In the open prairie it is quite another matter. On seeing a turkey or flock of them on a wide prairie, one can, by riding in a circuitous direction, as if passing in ignorance of them, get near and start them into a trot, and keep them trotting by keeping between them and the nearest timber. In this way, although you ride slowly, you will soon run them down. The first indication of exhaustion to be noted will be the dropping of their wings, and when the hunter sees that, he knows that they cannot rise to fly; he then closes in and easily rides the birds down. This is, or used to be, a favorite sport with the cowboys of Texas, in which they sometimes employed a lariat, catching the birds as they would a calf, or shooting them with a revolver. In case neither the revolver nor lariat is handy, they take a bullet, partly split with a knife, and then let the tip of their cow whiplash into the cleft of the bullet; clamping the lead tightly on the lash. Thus armed, they pursue the turkeys until they drop their wings, when, dashing among them, they strike the neck of the turkey with the lash, a foot from the end of the tip, which sends the bullet whizzing around the neck four to six times; and ere the turkey can recover, the cowboy dismounts and secures it.

If there is snow on the ground there is little trouble in following the turkeys by their tracks. I have done but little of such hunting, as sufficient snow seldom falls in the South to make good tracking. When you hunt turkeys on the snow, all there is to do is to find their tracks and follow them carefully until the birds are seen; then observe the same tactics as in stalking them on the bare earth.

In the South they are unprepared for much cold, and at such times will likely be found grouped together on the sunny slopes of hills, or behind

114

some log or fence, to avoid the bitter winds, especially if the sun is not shining. They will then often remain on their roosts half a day rather than alight on the cold snow.

If you attempt to stalk an old gobbler when he is gobbling it is quite easy if you learn the course he is taking and get ahead of him and simply wait. Some men hunt no other way and are successful; but it requires the greatest care, and a thorough knowledge of the woods you are in, so that you may take advantage of ridges, ravines, gulches, thickets, etc.

When you have discovered a flock of turkeys at some distance from you, stop and wait a few moments. If they are feeding, and you are unobserved by them, carefully note in what direction they are moving. It is hard to tell if they are going or coming two hundred yards away, but there is one way by which their movements can readily be determined and that is by their color. If they are approaching, you will notice the blackness of their breasts; or rather the birds will appear almost black; and if a majority so appear, you may be sure they are coming; in other words, if you see one or two of them straighten up, and they look quite dark or black, you can then be certain of their approach. On the other hand, if you notice that they look a lightish gray or brown color, they are going the other way. But do not be deceived, as sometimes a flock has stopped to feed, and they will be turning and facing in all directions while so engaged; occasionally one will straighten up, flop his wings, and look back. Have an eye to the band and you will see if many of them look black or gray. If there are gobblers in the bunch, note their breasts which are blacker than the hens.

There is another way to find the direction in which the turkeys are moving if you cannot see them. When you have found fresh signs in the woods, note the scratches carefully to see which way most of them incline. This is easily determined by the direction in which the leaves are thrown by the birds' feet. Sometimes, if the scratches are made late in the evening, they will look fresh the next morning and thus deceive the oldest hunter. I once saw scratches on an open pin oak and cane ridge; then others at twenty paces, and again at fifty paces still others. After a careful examination of the scratches, I concluded there must be two old gobblers that had made the signs; and, although I knew of twenty or thirty hens and some young gobblers on that ridge, I had no suspicion before that there were any old gobblers. Now, reader, what caused me to suspect from these scratchings that old gobblers were about, and that there were two of them was this: there were but few scratches and at long intervals. The scratches were very large, almost two feet across, while the leaves had been thrown five or six feet back, indicating long legs and large feet with a great stroke. I noticed there were two separate lines of scratches some ten feet apart on the main trend; also the scratches were twenty to fifty yards apart in the direction the birds were going, which indicated that the two birds were walking along at a brisk pace and keeping pretty well in a straight line, feeding as they went.

I believe no man alive or dead has killed more "old gobblers" than I have, and yet the heaviest I ever bagged weighed twenty-four pounds gross. This bird might have reached thirty or thirty-three pounds had he been fat, but it was late in the gobbling season, when the winter fat is run off by constant love affairs, leaving them greatly reduced in weight. This specimen was killed in Trinity County, Texas, where I have found the turkeys to average heavier than anywhere else I have hunted.

Audubon said the wild turkey would soon become extinct in the United States, sixty or seventy years ago; but to date his prophecy has failed in so far as the Southern or Gulf States are concerned. Although here as elsewhere hunted and persecuted without consideration, they are remarkably plentiful still. There are localities in the Gulf States that will not be cleared up or utilized for agricultural purposes in ages to come—if then. The immense swamps—annually overflowed—great hummocks, and the broken, untenable pine hills, will afford suitable retreats for the turkey for generations to come.

Wild turkeys are less understood by the average sportsman or even naturalist than any other of our game birds. It is common to read of the acute olfactory powers of the turkey; that he scents the hunter at one hundred to three hundred yards; the truth is it must be a pungent odor to have a turkey detect it at ten paces.

CHAPTER XVI
THE SECRET OF COOKING THE TURKEY

Of matters with which the average sportsman has to do, there is none so little understood as that of cooking game, and especially the turkey. Thousands of sportsmen go into the hunting camp expecting to play the rôle of cook without the knowledge of the simplest requirements and as a consequence are in perpetual trouble and disappointment on account of the blunders that are the inevitable results of lack of information. In the solitude of the forest the hunter should not be at loss for methods of cooking even if he has but a frying-pan; a log for a table; his plate, a section of bark or large leaf.

The turkey is supposed to be a bird of dry meat, but this is so only when all juices are boiled or baked out of it. The usual manner in which turkeys are cooked is by roasting or baking. If the turkey is an old one, the first process is to parboil until the flesh is tender; then it is stuffed with sundry things, such as bread-crumbs, oysters, shrimp, shallots, onions, garlic, truffles, red and black pepper, wine and celery to destroy the natural flavor of the bird. It is a mistake to disguise the rich, delicate flavor of turkey meat with the odor of fish, but it is done and called roast turkey.

If the turkey is a young one, cook it in the way usual to stove-baking, after first filling its cavity with a suitable dressing of bread-crumbs, pepper, salt, and onions chopped fine, moistened with fresh country butter. This is the best dressing that can be made, and will detract nothing from the flavor of the bird nor add to it. If an old turkey, parboil it until the flesh is quite tender, then stuff and bake.

In the forest camp I neither bake nor roast the turkey. Imagine a gobbler dressed and lying on a log or piece of bark beside you. Take a sharp knife, run the blade down alongside the keel bone, removing the flesh from one end of that bone to the other. By this process each half breast can be taken off in two pieces. Lay this slab of white meat skin side down, then begin at the thick end and cut off steaks, transversely, one half inch thick, until all the slab is cut. Now sprinkle with salt and pepper and pile the steaks up together; thus the salt will quickly penetrate. Do not salt any more than you want for one meal; the meat would be ruined if allowed to stand over for the next meal before cooking. Just as soon as the salt dissolves and the juice begins to flow, spread out the steaks in a pan, sprinkle dry flour lightly on both sides evenly, taking care to do this right, or you will get the flour on too thick. Give the pan a shake and the flour will adjust itself. This flour at once mixes with the juices of the meat, forming a crust around the steak, like batter. Have the frying-pan on the fire with plenty of grease, and sizzling hot so the steak will fry the moment it touches the hot grease. Put the steaks in until the bottom of the pan is covered, but never have one steak lap another. If the grease is quite hot the steak will soon brown, and when brown on one side, turn, and the moment it is brown on both sides take out of the pan. By this method you retain almost every particle of the juice of the meat, and at the same time it is brown and crisp, and will nearly melt in the mouth. The flour around the steak does not only prevent the escape of the juice, but also prevents any grease penetrating the meat. If you like gravy, have the frying-pan hot and about a teaspoonful of the grease in which the meat was fried left in it; take a half pint of cold water and pour into the pan. Let this boil about five minutes, when you will have a rich, brown gravy, which season with salt and pepper and pour hot over the steak. You don't want a thing else to eat except some good bread and a cup of creole coffee. Having eaten turkey thus cooked you would not care for baked or roast turkey again.

The bony portions of your turkey may be cut up at the joints, and all available put into a pot or saucepan having a lid, with a few slices of pork or bacon for seasoning, or fresh butter. No matter how fat any game is a little pork improves it. Put in a pod or two of red pepper and add a little water; let this boil and simmer until quite done. I am giving directions now for making a stew. For the thickening, take an onion or two and cut into small pieces, a pod of red pepper broken up, a tablespoonful of flour sifted, and some salt. Put all into a pan and pour in a cup of cold water, stir until the lumps of the flour disappear, then put the mixture into the pot with the turkey. Stir occasionally until it boils, and if there is not sufficient gravy in the vessel where the stew is cooking, add more water. Boil thirty minutes, then serve. In this stew you get the finest and most wholesome dish imaginable, and at very little expense and trouble.

There are many who can prepare food but never understand the reasons for doing things. Not one in a hundred knows why meal, flour, or cracker-crumbs are put on fish or meat while frying. They tell you it helps to brown the flesh; it does no such thing, but prevents browning while the meat is being cooked. Leave off the flour or meal, and by the time the meat is cooked it will be dry and hard as pine bark and as indigestible. When fish is rolled in flour or meal, the fish is not browned, but the covering is.

CHAPTER XVII
CAMERA HUNTING FOR TURKEYS

During the past ten years, while the season was open on wild turkeys, I have made a rule to leave the gun at home and hunt the turkey with the "camera" instead.

On countless occasions I have sat on the bank of a beautiful creek in Alabama watching and waiting for these noble birds to appear and pose. Time and patience, that's what it takes; likewise to know the ways of the bird.

On one occasion I had found their great tracks on the sandbank, and, noting it as a favorite crossing, made an impromptu blind to mask the camera lest the birds get the least glimpse of it or myself. It took me over two months to get an opportunity for the picture which I secured at last one afternoon as the sun was getting low. I had been calling at intervals, and just when least expected, there they were, moving slowly but watchfully toward the creek and across the scope of the lens. My finger was quick to reach the button as they stepped to the sandy bank, and turned to note that no enemy lurked behind. The click of the shutter startled them but little, and they walked quietly away. I knew I had a good negative, as the late afternoon sun shone brightly on their gorgeous plumage, and they were barely fifteen feet from where I sat.

Not one man in a million has ever had the opportunity of viewing one of these birds in life in the woods at ten to fifteen feet—nor ever will, and to these I hope the photographs will be a pleasure; for to see a ten-year-old gobbler so near, when he is not frightened—and you without gun or other means to injure him—so you may enjoy the most majestic bird the eye of man ever rested on, is not only a feast for the eye, but a pleasant memory that will be with you forever.

In November, 1899, in Alabama, I began to hunt with the camera, and for six months—with the exception of one day only, on which a terrific storm raged—not a day passed that I was not after turkey pictures, sometimes not seeing one in two or three weeks, then again encountering twenty-five to forty in one day. I spoiled several hundred plates in this time, snapping at every chance that occurred. There is no possibility of a time exposure on such sensitive birds, and one twenty-fifth of a second is scarcely quick enough. Often the click of the shutter, so like the snap of a gun when missing fire, sent them whirling into the air or scattered them, pellmell, afoot. I have stalked and crawled to their scratching places and sat concealed with camera masked on an old log or in a hollow stump, till sundown; all day, and the next and the next.

I have made three or four exposures in a day, gone home, developed the negatives, and found nothing on them but shadows—taken in shade; but at other times there was the just reward when all the plates came out with every image "perfect." Then, again, it would rain almost daily for a month or two. Still I went, camera slung over my shoulder, covered with a rubber sheet, hoping for sunshine.

Once I discovered a bearded hen and tried five weeks to catch her with the lens, and never saw her but twice during that time. The next season I found her again in company with three other hens. I called them within ten or twelve feet. This time it had been sunlight all day, but just a minute before they came near enough a thin haze covered the sun. Still, I pressed the button and got a dim negative of her and of one of her playmates, and have not seen her since.

To successfully photograph wild turkeys the greatest care must be taken in having a blind perfectly natural in appearance. Once in the blind, do not move; never mind the wind; wild turkeys cannot smell you any farther than you can them, but they can outsee anything except the heron, crane, and hawk, and you must get within fifteen or twenty feet of them in the bright sunshine, or no picture. Find their scratching places and hide behind a log, or make a blind of brush and green leaves, etc. Be sure to hide all the camera save the disk of the lens, and they will see that nearly every time. I have had them discover the lens and approach within two feet and peer at it with curious wonder, whine and purr, until satisfied it would not harm them, then walk serenely away.

At times when I saw a flock or an individual feeding at a distance, I would take my call and invite them to advance, "stand up and look pleasant," and if in the humor they would often comply. I have a friend living in New Orleans with whom a hundred happy hours have been spent in the camp, wild woods, and along the stream, chiefly in quest of these noble fowls. He and I have exchanged letters once a week for the past quarter of a century. Of course I regale him with every new photograph taken of turkeys. One day I mailed him several that set him afire, and on a certain day friend Renaud came to me with his old 10-gauge which has served him thousands of times.

The next morning when day broke we sat on the crest of a pine ridge adjacent to the hummock bordering the "Big-bee" river swamps, over which the turkeys roosted at night. Ere long the gray of the eastern horizon began to melt in to a rosy hue, and suddenly out of the deep swamp came the shrill, guttural but mighty pleasing "*Gil-obble-obble-obble*," of a turkey, echoing along the slopes and through the vales of the surrounding forests.

After a while we heard him gobble on the ridge, so I took my call and began to pipe a few words in turkey vernacular, which the old gentleman seemed to comprehend by the way he gave ready reply. By this time the turkeys had all flown down, several gobbling in as many directions. Several were approaching slowly, and we could hear them below the crest of the hill. Luck favored us, so far as nothing yet had disturbed them, and they gradually came nearer, until presently a remark from my companion, "Old Gobbler in sight?" "See him coming, two of them, yes, three"; and on they came, their great black breasts glowing in the bright sun, while their long beards swung from side to side.

Suddenly, when within thirty paces of us, one of them spied Renaud's new drab corduroy cap, which contrasted vividly with the black and charred log behind which we were hid, and "*Put,*" "*put;*" all were gone, helter-skelter.

Renaud's heart was broken—mine wrecked.

"Why in the d-dickens didn't you shoot?" I asked, mad as a hornet.

"I wanted to get them in position to get the two largest ones."

"Gee! you ought to have made sure of that fellow with the immense beard, and chance another on the rise or run;" but just as we were waxing into a fine quarrel, R. remarked in a whisper, "They are coming back."

"Yes," I replied, "and several others with them—some old ones and some yearlings; so make no mistake this time, and be sure of one of the old

122

ones."

They were very near now, and as I made a low call all stopped and some gobbled; then on they came in a careless manner, neither strutting nor exhibiting any special passion.

I quickly got in my camera work, and ducked my head in time to see the beautiful things walking away from the gun; then two well-measured reports—and the smoke clearing away showed two grand old patriarchs flopping over on the pine straw and soon lying still. I am not sure which was the proudest—I as *particeps criminis* or he as executioner.

THE END

THE COUNTRY LIFE PRESS
GARDEN CITY, N. J.

FOOTNOTES:

[1] Marsh, O. C. Proc. Acad. Nat. Sci., Phila., 1870, p. 11. Also Am. Jour. Sci., IV, 1872, 260. In a letter to me under date of April 25, 1912, Dr. George F. Eaton of the Museum of Yale University, New Haven, Conn., writes that "Type of *Meleagris altus* is in Peabody Museum with other types of fossil *Meleagris*." At the present writing I am not informed as to what these "other types" are; and I am writing of the opinion that the museum referred to by Doctor Eaton has no fossil meleagrine material that has not, up to date, been described. See also Amer. Nat., Vol. IV, p. 317.

Cope, E. D. "Synopsis of Extinct Batrachia, etc." *Meleagris superbus* (Trans. Amer. Philos. Soc., N. S. XIV, Pt. 1, 1870, 239). A long and careful description of *M. superbus* [superba] will be found here, where the species is said to be "established on a nearly perfect right tibia, an imperfect left one, a left femur with the condyles broken off, and a light coracoid bone, with the distal articular extremity imperfect."

[2] Shufeldt, R. W., "On Fossil Bird-Bones Obtained by Expeditions of the University of Pennsylvania from the Bone Caves of Tennessee." The Amer. Nat., July, 1897, pp. 645-650. Among those bones were many belonging to *M. g. silvestris*. Professor Marsh declined to allow me to even see the fossil bones upon which he based the several alleged new species of extinct *Meleagridæ* which he had described.

[3] Marsh, O. C. [Title on page 120.] *Meleagris antiqua.* Amer. Journ. Sci., ser. 3, II, 1871, 126. From this I extract the following description, to wit:—

Meleagris antiquus, sp. nov.

A large Gallinaceous Bird, approaching in size the wild Turkey, and probably belonging to the same group, was a contemporary of the *Oreodon* and its associates during the formation of the Miocene lake deposits east of the Rocky Mountains. The species is at present represented only by a few fragments of the skeleton, but among these is a distal end of a right humerus, with the characteristic portions all preserved. The specimen agrees in its main features with the humerus of *Meleagris gallopavo* Linn., the most noticeable points of difference being the absence in the fossil species of the broad longitudinal ridge on the inner surface of the distal end, opposite the radial condyle, and the abrupt termination of the ulnar condyle at its outer, superior border.

Measurements

Greatest diameter of humerus at distal end 12. lines Transverse diameter of ulnar condyle 3.4 " Vertical diameter of same 4. " Transverse diameter of radial condyle 4.25 "

The specimens on which this species is based were discovered by Mr. G. B. Grinnell of the Yale party, in the Miocene clay deposits of northern Colorado.

Ibid. IV, 1878, 261. [Title on p. 256.] "Art XXX. Notice of some new Tertiary and Post-Tertiary Birds." From this article by Professor Marsh I extract the following:

Meleagris celer, sp. nov.

A much smaller species of the same genus is represented by two tibiae and the proximal half of a tarso-metatarsal, which were found together, and probably belonged to the same individual. The tibia is slender, and has the shaft less flattened from before backward than in the last species [*M. altus*]. The distal half of the shaft has its anterior face more distinctly polygonal. From the head of the tibia a sharp ridge descends a short distance on the posterior face, where it is met by an external ridge of similar length. The tarso-metatarsal has the external ridge of the proximal end more prominent, and the posterior tendinal crest more ossified than in the larger species. The remains preserved indicate a bird about half the bulk of *M. altus*.

Measurements.

Length of tibia 183. mm Greatest diameter of proximal end 34. "

125

Transverse diameter of shaft at middle 9.6 " Transverse diameter of distal end 16.5 " Antero-posterior diameter of outer condyle 10. " Transverse diameter of proximal end of tarso-metatarsus 19. " Antero-posterior diameter 14. "

On page 260 is described *Meleagris altus*:

Meleagris altus [Marsh]. Proc. Phila. Acad. 1870, p. 11, and Amer. Nat., Vol. IV, p. 317. (*M. superbus* Cope, Synopsis Extinct Batrachia etc., p. 239.)

(Followed by description and the following measurements of the fossil bones.)

Length (approx.) of humerus 159.5 mm Greatest diameter proximal end 42. " Greatest diameter distal end 33. " Length of coracoid 122. " Transverse diameter of lower end 37.5 " Length of femur 150. " Transverse diameter of distal end 31. " Length of tibia 243. " Transverse diameter of distal end 18. " Length of tarso-metatarsus 176. " Transverse diameter of proximal end 23. " Distance from proximal end to spur 110. "

(A number of differences as compared with existing species are enumerated)

[4] Shufeldt, R. W. A Study of the Fossil Avifauna of the Equus Beds of the Oregon Desert. Journ. Acad. Nat. Sci., Phila., ser. 2, IX, 1892, pp. 389-425. Pls. XV-XVII. Advance abstracts of this memoir were published in The Auk (Vol. VIII, No. 4, October, 1891, pp. 365-368). The American Naturalist (Vol. XXV, No. 292, Apr., 1891, pp. 303-306, and *ibid.* No. 297, Sept., 1891, pp. 818-821) and elsewhere. Although no turkeys were discovered among these fossils, there were bones present of extinct grouse.

[5] Upon examining this material after it came into my hands, I found first, in a small tube closed with a cork, the distal end of the right humerus of some large bird. The cork was marked on the side, "Type," on top "*Mel. antiquus*. G. Ranch. Col. G. B. G. August 6, 1870." The specimen is pure white, thoroughly fossilized, and imperfect. The second of the two specimens received is in a small pasteboard box, marked on top "Birds. Meleagris, sp. nov. N. J., *Meleagrops celer* (type)." The specimen is the imperfect, proximal moiety of the left tarso-metatarsus of a rather large bird. It is thoroughly fossilized, earth-brown in color, with the free borders of the proximal end considerably worn off. On its postero-external aspect, written in ink, are the

words "*M. celer.*"

[6] In making this statement, I take the words of Dr. Geo. Bird Grinnell as written on the cork of the bottle containing the specimen to be correct, and not the locality given elsewhere. (The A. O. U. Check-List of North American Birds. Third Edition, 1910, p. 388.) Moreover, the specimen is pure white, which is characteristic of the fossils found in the White River region of Colorado. This is confirmed by Professor Marsh in his article quoted above.

[7] Shufeldt, R. W. "Osteological Studies of the Subfamily Ardeinæ." Journ. Comp. Med. and Surg., Vol. X, No. 4, Phila., October, 1889, pp. 287-317.

[8] Shufeldt, R. W. Amer. Nat, July. 1897. p. 648. I have had no occasion to change my opinion since.

[9] Audubon, J. J. "The Birds of America," Vol. V, pp. 54-55. Even in Audubon's time the wild turkeys were being rapidly exterminated. At this time *M. g. silvestris* does not occur east of central Pennsylvania.

[10] Columella. (*De Re Rustica*, VIII, cap. 2.) Edwards (*Gleanings*, II, p. 269). 1760?

[11] Newton, Alfred. *A Dictionary of Birds.* (Assisted by Hans Gadow, with contributions from Richard Lydekker, Chas. S. Roy, and Robert W. Shufeldt, M. D.) Pt. IV, 1896, p. 994. The quotation is from the Art. "Turkey," and in further reference to its name, Professor Newton remarks, "The French *Coq* and *Poule d'Inde* (whence *Dindon*) involve no contradiction, looking to the general idea of what India then was. One of the earliest German names for the bird, *Kalekuttisch Hüm* (whence the Scandinavian *Kalkun*) must have arisen through some mistake at present inexplicable; but this does not refer, as is generally supposed, to Calcutta, but to Calicut on the Malabar coast (Notes and Queries, ser. 6, X, p. 185).

"But even Linnæus could not clear himself of the confusion, and, possibly following Sibbald, unhappily misapplied the name *Meleagris*, undeniably belonging to the guinea-fowl, as the generic term for what we now know as the turkey, adding thereto as its specific designation the word *gallopavo*, taken from the *Gallopavus* of Gesner, who, though not wholly free from error, was less mistaken than some of his contemporaries and even successors."

[12] Baird, Spencer F. *The Origin of the Domestic Turkey*. Rep. of the Comm. of Agricul. for the year 1866. Washington Gov. Printing Office, 1867, pp. 288-290. In this article Professor Baird undertakes to demonstrate "that there are two species of wild turkey in North America; one confined to the more eastern and southern United States, the other to the southern Rocky Mountains and adjacent part of Texas, New Mexico, and Arizona; that the latter extends along eastern Mexico as far south at least as Orizaba, and that it is from this Mexican species and not from that of eastern North America that this domestic turkey is derived." [Reprinted in Hist. of N. Amer. Birds, III, p. 411, footnote.]

[13] Bennett, E. T. "The Gardens and Menagerie of the Zoölogical Society delineated." [The Drawings by William Harvey; Engr. by Branston and Wright, assisted by other artists] London, 1835. Further on, this article will be quoted on other points, as it treats of the entire history of the wild turkey.

[14] In the original work, here quoted, names of persons and some other nouns are printed in capitals—an old custom which publishers of the present work decided not to follow. My MS. was made to agree with the original in all particulars. R. W. S.

[15] Pennant, Thos. Esqr. F. R. S. "An Account of the Turkey." Phil. Trans. of the Royal Society of London. Vol. LXXI for the year 1781. London [Art.] No. 1. Communicated by Joseph Banks, Esqr., P. R. S. Read December 21, 1781, pp. 77, 78.

Pennant's contribution fills a large place in the literature of the wild turkey, and further on I shall take occasion to quote still more extensively from it. It starts in by giving in brief the characters of the turkey, and in describing the wild turkey he cites the previous works of Josselyn (Voyage); Clayton (Virginia); Catesby, Belon, Gesner, Aldrovandus, Ray, Buffon, and others. He gives a "Description" of the bird, especially the "Tail," and adds that a "White Turkey"—"A most beautiful kind has of late been introduced into England of a snowy whiteness, finely contrasting with its red head. These I think came from Holland, probably bred from an accidental white pair; and from them preserved pure from any dark or variegated birds." (p.

68.)

He presents variation in "Size," quoting Josselyn (New-Eng. Rarities); Lawson (History of Carolina); and Clayton (Phil. Trans.). Also their "Manners"; their being "Gregarious"; "Their Haunts," "Place," and much else, having more to do with their habits than their history, and consequently not legitimately to be touched upon in this chapter.

[16] Coues, Elliott. "History of the Wild Turkey." *Forest and Stream*, XIII, January 1, 1879, p. 947.

Another work I have examined on this part of our subject is D. G. Elliot's "Game Birds of America," and the turkey cuts in this book were copied by Coues into the last edition of his "Key to North American Birds," and very poorly done. Dr. D. G. Elliot's superb work, illustrated by magnificent colored plates by the artist Wolfe, on "A Monograph of the Phasianidæ or the Family of the Pheasants," I have not examined. The copy in the Library of Congress was out on a loan when I made application for it. Several plates of different species of wild turkeys are to be found in it.

[17] Pennant's article is illustrated by a folding plate giving the leg of a turkey bearing a supernumery toe situated in front of the tibiotarsus with the claw above. The note in reference to it is here reproduced in order to complete the article. Philos. Trans., Vol. LXXI, Ab. III, p. 80:

"To this account I beg leave to lay before you the very extraordinary appearance on the thigh of a turkey bred in my poultry yard, and which was killed a few years ago for the table. The servant in plucking it was very unexpectedly wounded in the hand. On examination the cause appeared so singular that the bird was brought to me. I discovered that from the thigh-bone issued a short upright process, and to that grew a large and strong toe, with a sharp and crooked claw, exactly resembling that of a rapacious bird."

[18] Bartram, William. Travels through North and South Carolina, Georgia, East and West Florida, the Cherokee Country, the Extensive Territories of the Muscogalges or Creek Confederacy, and the Country of the Choctaws. Containing an account of the soil and Natural Productions of those regions; together with the observations on the manners of the Indians. Embellished with Copper Plates.

The original edition of Bartram is cited in the *Third Instalment of American Ornithological Bibliography* by Elliott Coues (the references being pp. 83 and 290 *bis*). Bull. U. S. Geol. and Geogr. Surv. Terr. 1879, p. 810, Govm't Printing Office. It is here in this work of his that Bartram designates the domestic turkey as *Meleagris gallopavo*, Linn.; and the wild turkey of this country (*M. occidentalis*) (p. 83) as *M. americanus* (p. 290 *bis*).

[19] Barton, P. S. *The Philadelphia Medical and Physical Journal*, Vol. II, 1806, pp. 162-164. Coues, in his *Ornitho. Biblio.*, cited above, omits the words, "The Philadelphia," which gives trouble to find the work in a library; he also has the year wrong, giving 1805 for 1806—the latter being correct. The copy I consulted had no Pl. 1, with the article, that I happened to see.

[20] Clinton, De Witt. *Trans. Lit. and Philos. Soc.*, New York, 1, 1815, pp. 21-184. Note S. pp. 125-128.

[21] Owen, R. P. Z. S., V. 1837, pp. 34, 35.

[22] Le Conte, John. *Proc. Acad. Nat. Sci. of Phila.* IX, 1857, pp. 179-181. The distinctive characters and the habits, as given by this author of the wild and domesticated turkeys of the United States, are doubtless of some value; but the deductions he draws from the comparisons made are, as we know, quite erroneous. I have not examined the article by E. Roger in the *Bull. Soc. Acclim.* cited by Coues in his *Ornitho. Biblio.* as having appeared in the "2c Ser. VII, 1870, pp. 264-266." Either the year or the pagination, or both, of the citation is wrong, and as many of the copies were out at the time of my search, and the others distributed through several libraries, I failed to obtain it. R. W. S.

[23] Gould, J. 2. On a new turkey, *Meleagris Mexicana.* P. Z. S. XXIV, 1856, pp. 61-63. (In his *Ornithol. Bibliogr.*) Coues remarks upon this as follows: "Subsequently determined to be the stock whence the domestic bird descended, and hence a synonym of *M. gallopavo*, Linn."

This paper was extensively republished at the time, generally under the title of "A new species of turkey from Mexico" [all citing the P. Z. S. article]. One journal quoted it as follows: "Mr. Gould exhibited a specimen of turkey which he had obtained in Mexico, and which differed materially from the wild turkey of the United States. At the same time this turkey so closely resembled the domesticated turkey of Europe that he believed naturalists were wrong in attributing its origin to the United States species. The present specimen was therefore a new species, and he proposed to call it *Meleagris Mexicana*, which, if his theory was correct, must henceforth be the designation of the common turkey." Amer. Jour. Sci. XXII, 1856, p. 139. Under the same title this latter was reprinted in Edinb. *New Philos. Journ.* n. s., iv, 1856, pp. 371, 372. See also Bryant, H. "*Remarks on the supposed new species of turkey, Meleagris Mexicana, recently described by Mr. Gould.*" Proc. Bost. Soc. Nat. Hist. vi, 1857, pp. 158, 159. "In the Proceedings of the Zoölogical Society of London for 1856, page 61," says Professor Baird, "Mr. Gould characterizes as new a wild turkey from the mines of Real del Norte, in Mexico, under the name of *Meleagris Mexicana*, and is the first to suggest that it is derived from the domesticated bird, and not from the common wild turkey of eastern North America, on which he retains the name of *M. gallopavo*, of Linnæus. He stated that the peculiarities of the new species consist chiefly in the creamy white tips of the tail feathers and of the upper tail coverts, with some other points of minor importance. I suggest that the wild turkey of New Mexico, as referred to by various writers, belongs to this new species, and not to the *M. gallopavo*." (loc. cit. p. 289.) Compare the above with what Professor Baird states in the series of the *Pacif. Railroad Reports*, vol. ix, p. 618, with the remainder of the above quoted article, which is too long to reproduce here.

[24] Bennett, E. T. "Publ. with the sanction of the council under the superintendence of the Secretary and Vice Secretary of the Society. Birds. Vol. II. London, 1835, pp. 209-224." There is a very excellent wood-cut of a turkey illustrating this article (left lateral view), of which the author says: "Our own figure is taken from a young male, in imperfect plumage, brought from America by Mr. Audubon. Another specimen, in very brilliant plumage, but perhaps not purely wild, forms a part of the Society's Museum" (p. 223). Bennett derived most of his information about the habits of the wild turkey in nature "from an excellent memoir by M. Charles Lucien Bonaparte, in his continuation of Wilson's American Ornithology."

"In that work M. Bonaparte claims credit for having given the first representation of the wild turkey;* and justly so, for the figures introduced into a landscape in the account of De Laudonniere's Voyage to Florida in De Bry's Collection, and that published by Bricknell in his Natural History of

North Carolina, cannot with certainty be referred to the native bird. They are besides too imperfect to be considered as characteristic representations of the species. Much about the same time with M. Bonaparte's figure appeared another, in M. Viellot's Galerie des Oiseaux, taken from a specimen in the Paris Museum.

"It is somewhat singular that so noble a bird, and in America at least by no means a rare one, should have remained unfigured until within five years of the present time; all the plates in European works being manifestly derived from domestic specimens." Bennett was aware that Audubon's Plates were published about this time, for he mentions them. He also was well informed in matters regarding the crossing of the wild male turkey with the female domestic one, and with the improvement in the breed thus obtained.

* Note: Newton disputes this and says: "In 1555 both sexes were characteristically figured by Belon (Oiseaux, p. 249), as was the cock by Gesner in the same year, and these are the earliest representations of the bird known to exist." (Dict. of Birds, pp. 995, 996.)

[25] Newton states that this assertion "is wholly untrustworthy," as carp, pickerel (and other commodities) both lived in this country (England) long before 1524, "if indeed they were not indigenous to it." (Dict. of Birds, p. 995).

[26] No two authors seem to agree upon the exact date when the turkey was really introduced into England. Here Bennett states positively 1530; Professor Baird has it 1541; Alfred Newton 1524, and so on.

[27] Leland's Collectanea, (1541).

[28] *Dugdale*. "Origines Juridiciales."

[29] Shufeldt, R. W. "The Ancestry of the American Turkey," *Shooting and Fishing*, Vol. 24, No. 13, New York, July 14, 1898, p. 246. "Wild and Domesticated Turkeys," *Ibid*. No. 17, August 11, 1898, p. 331. "A Reply to the Turkey Hunters," *Ibid*. No. 23, September 22, 1898, pp, 451, 452. "The Wild Turkey of Arizona," *Ibid*. Vol. 32, No. 5, New York, May 22, 1902, pp. 108, 109.

[30] Nelson, E. W. "Description of a New Subspecies of *Meleagris gallopavo* and proposed changes in the nomenclature of certain North American birds." Auk, XVII, April 1900, pp. 120-123.

[31] Among the luxuries belonging to the high condition of civilization exhibited by the Mexican nation at the time of the Spanish conquest was the possession of Montezuma by one of the most extensive zoölogical gardens on record, numbering nearly all the animals of that country, with others brought at much expense from great distances, and it is stated that turkeys were supplied as food in large numbers daily to the beasts of prey in the menagerie of the Mexican Emperor. (Baird, *ibid.* pp. 288, 289.)

[32] Ogilvie-Grant, W. R. "A Hand-book to the Game-Birds." (Lloyd's Nat. Hist., London, 1897, pp. 103-111.) Genus *Meleagris*. Describes briefly some of the North American Turkeys, and also *M. ocellata* (full page colored figure). Nest and eggs of all described in brief.

[33] Michaux, F. "Travels in N. Amer." 1802 Eng. Trans., p. 217. See also the following: Blyth, E., "Ann. and Mag. of Nat. Hist.," 1847, vol. xx., p 391. This author points out that these turkeys in India are flightless, black in color, small, and the appendage over the bill of great size.

[34] Dixon, E. S. "Ornamental Poultry," 1818, p. 34. This author also noted the interesting fact that the female of the domesticated turkey sometimes has the tuft of hair on her breast like the male. Bechstein refers to the old German fable or superstition that a hen turkey lays as many eggs as the gobbler has feathers in the under tail-coverts, which, as we know, vary in number. (Naturgesch. Deutschlands, B iii, 1793, s. 309.).

[35] "Gardener's Chronicle," 1852, p. 699.

[36] Darwin, Charles. "Animals and Plants Under Domestication," Vol. 1, 1868, pp. 352-355. Other facts of this character are set forth here which are of interest in the present connection.

[37] Darwin, Charles. "The Origin of Species," 1880, pp. 70, 158. He also shows that the young of wild turkey are instinctively wild.

[38] Woodhouse, Dr. (Amer. Nat. vii, 1873, p, 326.).

[39] Henshaw, H. W. Rept. Geogr. and Geol. Expl. and Surv. West of the 100th meridian. 1875. Chap. III. The Ornith. Coll. 1871-1874, p. 435.

[40] Caton, J. D. "The Wild Turkey and Its Domestication." Amer. Nat. xi, No. 6, 1877, pp. 321-330, also *Ibid.* vii, 1873, where this author states that "The vision of the wild turkey is very acute but the sense of smell is very dull." (p. 431.)

133

[41] Bendire, Charles, "Life Histories of North American Birds with Special Reference to Their Breeding Habits and Eggs." Washington, Govmt. Printing Office, 1892.

[42] Some of the English books contain descriptions of the eggs of our wild turkeys, as for example "A Hand-book to the Game-birds." By W. R. Ogilvie-Grant. (Lloyd's Nat. Hist.) London, 1897, pp. 103-111.

[43] Shufeldt, R. W. "Osteology of Birds," Education Dept. Bull. No. 447, Albany, N. Y., May 15, 1909. N. Y. State Mus. Bull. 130, pp. 222-224; based upon a former contribution which appeared in *The Journal of Comparative Medicine and Surgery*, July, 1887, entitled "A Critical Comparison of a Series of Skulls of the Wild and Domesticated Turkeys." (*Meleagris gallopavo silvestris* and *M. domestica.*)